WAS IT ALL FOR NOTHING?

WAS IT ALL FOR NOTHING?

Finding Purpose Through Trauma

MELISSA SANDERS

Trilogy Christian Publishers

A Wholly Owned Subsidiary of Trinity Broadcasting Network

2442 Michelle Drive

Tustin, CA 92780

10 9 8 7 6 5 4 3 2 1

Library of Congress Cataloging-in-Publication Data is available.

ISBN 978-1-64773-486-2

ISBN 978-1-64773-487-9 (ebook)

Dedication

First and foremost, I give all glory to God for birthing this book. Thank You for Your goodness always. I dedicate this book to God for being my strength, to Jesus for being my friend, and to the Holy Spirit for being my helper.

To my husband, James, next to our Father in heaven, I dedicate this book to you. Thank you for your unwavering strength and support from the very beginning and constantly encouraging me. I also dedicate this book to my three children, Eva, Drew, and Ellie. Thank you for your unwavering love and support through it all. Without your help, this project would never have been finished. To Ellie, the Lord saved you for a purpose, and I cannot wait to see how He uses you in every area of your life. To Eva and Drew, the discernment the Lord has instilled into you is such a blessing, and I pray that you continually lean into our Lord for everything.

Table of Contents

Preface

After experiencing a traumatic event with my youngest daughter, which resulted in anxiety, panic, depression, and PTSD, I had a radical encounter with the Holy Spirit, who, in an instant, delivered me from all that I was being oppressed from. I received emotional, physical, and spiritual healing in an instant, and that encounter changed my life forever.

The Lord spoke to me and told me He was going to anoint me to write a book and to tell our story (of me and the Holy Spirit) so that others could also receive healing from past traumatic events that had left a stronghold over them in some way. The Lord desires His children to be restored, healed, and made whole through the blood of Jesus Christ, and He longs for an intimate relationship with His daughters who have lost their identity.

The burden placed on my heart was to learn who I was and whom I belonged to, to figure out what that meant. The instructions from there were to teach others how to get back into alignment or to find their true identity for the very first time. I have been a follower of Christ all my life, and all that unfolded spiritually after this traumatic event started the unraveling process of a lot of religious beliefs that needed to be dismantled. The chapter outline that the Holy Spirit gave to me stretched me in every way possible. I had to confront lifelong belief systems that were not from Him, and I had to submit and be open to learning something new about the Lord, regardless of how it would be perceived from the faith community. The Lord also gave me the ability to paint, and I pray that as you read the chapters and study the paintings that accompany each one, you will feel God's love for you.

The first three chapters were the most difficult for me to write, and it took me the longest amount of time. This is partially because it contains my testimony, and reliving those events was really emotional. Another reason is because the Lord was asking me to teach on the Bible. I went to school to be a nurse, and I felt very inadequate in going deep into the scriptures as I have not received any formal teaching on the Bible. A lot of research and my own personal study needed to take place, as well as getting to a place with the Lord for Him to teach me what He wanted me to know and what to say. After I received my approval from Trilogy Publishers that they were offering me a contract to complete this project, it all seemed to fall into place as it needed to. I have three small children at home and a husband who works, so it really was a family-birthed book as they gave me the time and space on my husband's days off to really plow through and finish. I was able to get my first draft of a completed copy of this book done in seven weeks! That might not be great to a seasoned writer, but from someone who has a more science-oriented background, I am going to take that as a great feat. All glory to God for that!

This project has taught me so much about my own personal relationship with God, and I am so thankful for all that was and is to come as you read it. I pray abundant blessings over you and that the Lord will touch you in a new way as you navigate through each chapter. Amen.

Introduction

I never in my life dreamed that I would write a book. It was not ever anything that I daydreamed about or sought any career in. I love to read, and I am an incredibly fast reader, but I have always been more of a math and science person. Professionally, I went on to be a registered nurse, receiving a bachelor's degree in a field of science. I am not a theologian, I did not go to Bible college, and I have never been in church ministry. So why on earth would you listen to me? I am an everyday person who was blessed, rescued, and saved by God, and He instructed me to tell my story—to tell our story—to bring Him glory and honor from everyday people.

I wanted to briefly address mental health concerns. Hear my heart here. I am not devaluing any individual situation, condition, or diagnosis. This book is certainly not a how-to list of things that you should do to magically cure anything. I know that the complexity of mental health cannot be solved in the pages here, and in no way am I attempting to do that. This book is about dealing with the aftermath of a traumatic event that leads to emotional disturbances specifically related to that event, along with where God fits into the whole scenario. It was only after going through a similar situation that I realized that many people, specifically women, are suffering in silence from the tragic events or experiences in their own lives. All for very individual reasons.

Parenting is the most difficult, excruciating, exhausting, rewarding, and joyful experience I have ever had in my life. It opens and exposes your soul to the world where your impressionable and vulnerable little ones are running around. This in turn can lead to your own vulnerabilities, as we cannot control anything. If you are a parent, maybe you have had similar feelings or fears, or if you are like me, the vulnerability seemed to be a constant reminder of the possibility of failure or loss, creating a blanket of fear. Life can change in an instant, and oftentimes we tend to dwell on the possibility of bad things happening, which causes us to miss the joy found in the journey. That is what the Lord whispered to me as I was reeling with the trauma of nearly losing my child. I will tell you a little more about that, but first I would like to invite you on a journey to find the faith to trust in your heavenly Father in all things. Even if you are in excruciating pain and despair right now, there is a Comforter ready to help you, to bring truth, healing, and joy into your life. We all have different experiences, different values, and different responses to trauma, and telling my story is in no way an attempt to compare my experience to any of yours. We encounter trauma all the time, and sometimes the suffering that we endure does not directly affect us or our family members, but it might be as a bystander witnessing a tragic event, or a difficult set of circumstances that someone else is experiencing. The manifestations of our emotions or how our body processes trauma does not always make sense. Do not read my story as the apex of trauma. There are people around me who have suffered far greater losses or have been through more horrific events than I experienced. What God showed me about telling my story is that no matter what you have been through, or how great the climb has been, or how low the valley has been—He knows. He paid for your pain on the cross, and He is the One who can take your pain, loss, and turmoil, changing it for the good in your life.

During my time with the Lord just a year prior to beginning this book, a thought that would never have originated from me entered my spirit that said, *"I am anointing you to write books."* I said, "Lord, clearly You have the wrong person!" If you have ever been in a debate with God before, you probably know how that ends up, so here I am! I have sat and wrestled with the thought of writing my story for so long because it seems to be the popular thing to do these days. Everyone seems to be writing books, and I just did not believe that anyone would care to read what I would have to write—until God corrected me. He told me that the intention of this book is to break chains, bring deliverance, and save others who have gone through trauma. This book is a testament to His goodness, His might, His power, and His never-ending love for me—and for you. My given mission for this project was to help you understand how loved you are and to come to an unabashed, reckless, abandoned, makes-no-sense understanding of who God truly is and what He thinks about you, His precious and darling daughters.

I would love to take this opportunity to pray for you right now. As you read the following prayer, I invite you to open your heart and receive God's love for you. Even if you do not believe that you can get to a place of wholeness in your current circumstances, God has already spoken that over you. The fight has already been won. When I was in my darkest hour, it was very difficult to see the light at the end, but I kept pressing in—even if out of sheer desperation. Allow these words to soak over you so you may receive and understand your full identity, even on the bad days. Bless you, friends.

Father. I thank You for the trials because that is where You showed Yourself to me. I pray for every individual who is reading this now or is being thought of by a person reading these words. You have already won the victory over trauma, emotional disturbances, anxiety, depression, panic, and shame, no matter what the root is, and You bought that victory with Your blood. Father, right now I pray for hearts to be open and willing to know You. You lift the bondage, break the chains, and free Your people from past hurts/experiences/turmoil that have laid a foundation for them to feel shattered and unhinged. I declare Psalm 147:3 over Your people; heal the brokenhearted and bind up their wounds now, in the name of Jesus. Let the words in this book be Your words. May you be elevated and lifted up higher and higher until the final page. In Your mighty name, amen.

RESURRECTION POWER

"Why is it thought incredible by any of you that God raises the dead?"

—*Acts 26:8 ESV*

Of all of the challenging concepts presented in the Bible, God raising the dead has stretched my ability to comprehend His ways greater than any other. I work in healthcare and have both witnessed and been involved in attempts to bring a stopped heart back to life through lifesaving measures. You would think that this would increase my faith in God raising the dead. Sometimes CPR works, and sometimes it does not. Medicine has made so many incredible advancements throughout history, so I guess my reliance had been placed in human ability. Nothing, not even medicine, can surpass the One who created life. If He created man out of dust, surely He could raise a life from the dead. We read stories in the Bible about ten people, including Jesus, who were raised from the dead through supernatural measures, but does He still do that today?

My Testimony

We have three wonderful children. It never occurred to us that we would have three kids. In fact, we thought we were done having children after two. We had a daughter, followed by a son, and starting over with a pregnancy, then middle-of-the-night feedings and all that goes into raising a child just was not something we thought we were ready for. We had to try really hard for our first two pregnancies. I had been diagnosed with poly cystic ovarian syndrome before my husband and I got married, and every other month I would go through excruciating pain as my body would rupture a cyst. The doctor told me that it would be difficult, if not impossible, for me to conceive a child naturally. Okay, let us pause for a moment. Have you ever had a bad medical report before? I appreciate doctors and their ability to see a problem or disease process and use tools to assist the body in restoration. However, I also believe that medical professionals should think about the weight of their words in a greater way for the impact that they carry. "*The tongue can bring death or life; those who love to talk will reap the consequences*" (Prov. 18:21 nlt). I believe we will all answer to our heavenly Father for the words we have spoken. Have they been spoken to edify, encourage, and exalt, even in the midst of a dire reality? Or have they been spoken from a hopeless space in the constraints of protocols and procedures? I realize that speaking the truth about a medical report is important, but helping the patient find hope is important, too, and where to find that hope is a missing concept in that line of work. This is what I witnessed a lot in the hospital. There are not a lot of great reports given within those four walls. The reality is, God is greater than every other name. He is greater than any disease, but He is not typically welcome in the clinical space.

Sorry for the tangent, but I did partner with the negative report that my body wouldn't be able to conceive a child naturally. After a few months of attempts, I went straight to interventions instead of pressing in and seeking God for more answers and His plan. After the maximum number of rounds of each fertility method, we decided to wait and see what God wanted to do. Interventions beyond what we partnered to do are extremely invasive and expensive, so we decided to pause. Lo and behold, we got pregnant the very next month. We naturally conceived our son as well, although we had to be very intentional with the tracking and monitoring of fertility signs. We tried for about a year with our second pregnancy, but we had the blessing of a healthy and perfect son. We were so full and complete in heart with our family of four. For all the work that went into bringing these children into this world, we were elated and felt peaceful about having completed our family.

About fourteen months later, I was standing in the kitchen and my oldest, who was about four years old at the time, came up to me, rubbed my tummy, and said, "Mommy, I just love that baby that you are growing in your tummy." My first reaction was to tell her that no, Mommy was not growing a baby in her tummy. Then on the inside, I cringed a little because I was still a little overweight from having my son over a year earlier, and I was feeling very self-conscious about that. Bless these children who are so innocent with their words— they mean no hurt. So, I rationalized her statement with the extra weight that I carried on my body and immediately made a pact in my mind that I would get more serious about getting down to a healthier weight. Two weeks later, I looked at the calendar and had a sinking feeling. I immediately went out and bought a pregnancy test. Positive. How did my daughter know that? My husband and I just sat in shock and processed every emotion that was possible. When we told our kids that Mommy was going to have another baby, our daughter responded with, "Yeah, I told you that. It is a girl." I assured her that it was too soon to find out the baby's gender and that it would be several months before we would know for sure. At our twenty-week anatomy scan, the tech told us that we were having a girl, and our daughter seemed really annoyed. When we asked her what was wrong, she said, "I already told you guys that!" It was at this moment I realized that God was speaking to her.

This pregnancy was my most difficult. I was what they called "advanced maternal age" at thirty-six years old. I could not keep any food down; I lost fifteen pounds and did not gain any weight. It was my longest labor and the most painful, but just like every pregnancy I experienced, the moment I held my baby girl in my arms, it became all worth it. She was a gift that I did not know that I needed, but God did.

When she was five weeks old, an event occurred that is the entire reason for the journey I have been on, the only reason this book even exists. Even when I talk about it today, I refer to it is as "THE THING." My husband is a firefighter/paramedic, and when he left for work that morning, I was supposed to be heading to meet my mom so she could take the older two kids for a few days. I fed the baby and put her down for a nap in my bed, then went downstairs to go feed the older two and get them ready to leave. When I heard the baby crying upstairs, I paused to assess whether it was an immediate need or if she could work it out herself. She stopped mid-cry, and I felt the sense to go check on her, but I started to talk myself out of it. I said things to myself like, "Oh, she figured it out, maybe she just put herself back to sleep." I then had a very loud voice in my head yell, "*GO NOW!*" I ran as fast as I could to check on her, and when I entered my room, I found her facedown, not breathing, and lifeless. She had rolled in my bed, and her face was caught in my bedsheets. She was unable to turn her head like she normally did when she was on her stomach. As I remember those moments, they replay in my mind like a movie. Somehow it doesn't seem real. As I was sitting and pondering, watching the movie play of this moment in time, I can see the horror and panic rising in me. I started to breathe very fast, shallow breaths. My daughter's body was as white as my sheets; she was unresponsive, with no reflexes present. I undressed her, but I was not able to think enough to check her pulse. I just started to do strong sternal rubs on her. I can see Jesus standing next to me as I cry out, "Oh, God, MAKE HER BREATHE!" Then she let out a gasp for air. She was slowly recovering after that breath, but she kept going in and out of consciousness. I called my husband at that time and immediately asked him to come with the ambulance. While I was waiting for him to arrive, I just kept hearing the same words in my mind, *Anoint her with oil and speak life into her.* Those words repeated in my mind. In my desperation, I looked about my room and saw a bottle of frankincense essential oil on the changing table. I put two drops of oil into my palm and anointed her feet, her spine, and the crown of her head as I said, "You are going to be fine." Internally I did not think or believe that. In fact, I was shaking, I was so incredibly scared. However, something happened that is nothing short of miraculous. I witnessed her feet turning pink from where I put oil on her feet, and I watched as from her feet up to her head, her body turned pink again, her reflexes returned, and the light in her eyes returned. She was able to make eye contact again and track me. I had studied the power of essential oils for five years to that point. The organic chemistry and the physiology of its benefits in the body is a subject I am extremely passionate about and intrigued by. As I reflect back on those precious moments, it is not a surprise that God used something tangible that my brain could comprehend and understand.

My husband and his partner came in with the monitors and got our daughter all hooked up. Besides her temperature being slightly low, her vitals were stable and normal. Even after two and a half years and typing this story out, it still brings me right back to those moments as if it was yesterday. I just wept typing these words, not because I am still in that place of shock and trauma, but because of the power that God has, the tools and creativity of how He chooses to work in moments to partner with us, and how He loves us so much. I will always be wrecked by His loving-kindness.

So, does He still raise the dead? I can tell you one absolute truth. He raised two lives from death that day.

The Aftermath

What I have learned through sharing my story—even if it has only been part of it thus far—is the power of the testimony. We all have situations that we have been through that God wants to use to bring healing to others. I know I am not alone, because as I started sharing my story I would get messages from women saying that they were thankful I had shared because they had been through a really hard situation, too, and they were not brave enough to share. This provided me with more bravery and courage to begin to share my struggle, not necessarily about the initiating event, but about the downward emotional spiral in the aftermath, and it has had the ability to shine light into those dark places. The truth is, I have always only told a partial version of this story to others, even to those close to me. I never told anyone that I was hearing voices and responding to them, or that I had an out-of-body experience and witnessed Jesus breathe life back into my baby, but it still brought encouragement to others dealing with similar pain. When I was sitting with God about writing this, I knew that it was time to tell the full story. In the full story, you can see how powerful God is.

I have been a believer for thirty-three years, but I was never taught the power and intercession that God imparts into our daily lives. Maybe I was extremely behind the theological bar, or just naïve to who God really is, to believe that He would care about my day-to-day, seemingly insignificant aspects of my life. I have read about wonders, signs, and miracles in the Bible, but I did not necessarily think they still happened today. I just had never experienced anything like that before in my life. I thought I was going crazy, and I could not think to bring anyone else in on that experience for fear they would find me to be crazy, as well.

There is a real enemy in this world that only comes to steal, kill, and destroy, and he is looking for a sliver of doubt in all of us to take root so that he can engage in an epic battle of the mind. I was immediately attacked in my mind after this event. Instead of rejoicing in the fact that God had made Himself known to me, had given my baby back to me, and wanted me to lean into Him, I started to immediately have feelings of deep despair, hopelessness, fear, worry, shame, depression, and panic. By nature, I am a pretty walled-off person. I am not 100 percent an introvert, but I get "peopled out" very easily. I need alone time with God to refill my cup, and after this event took place, my cup was covered in puncture holes. Also, in all honesty, everything I experienced was so new that I started to question everything I had ever believed or been taught about God. Every time I attempted to be filled back up, it would immediately pour out. All the things that I had built as protection methods were shattered. I felt exposed, as if all of my nerve endings were raw. Have you ever had a nerve issue in a tooth? Something hot or cold touches it, and it immediately sends an electric feeling of pain? That is the best way I can describe how every inch of my body felt. I felt like that whenever someone touched me when I was not prepared for it. How difficult and awful of a feeling is that to have when you have three young children who constantly want to touch you? I felt like a failure as a parent. Loud noises were a big trigger for me, and I would need to lock myself in the bathroom to calm myself down. Of all the inward torment I was going through, the one external manifestation of it is something that I have held the most shame about were my outbursts of anger. They started out as something I could control, but they eventually became a force on their own, and sadly, I hurt many people during this time. People whom I loved the most seemed to be in the crosshairs, and all the willpower in the world was not working anymore. I did every Bible study I could get my hands on to curb my angry outbursts, but it appeared nothing was working.

The people who were the closest to me did not understand, and frankly, I was filled with so much shame that I isolated myself, thinking I was doing everyone a favor by staying away, but that caused a lot of hurt along the way, as well. I could not allow anyone into the darkness that I felt. Each time I tried to visit those places, an overwhelming amount of sorrow would fill me, and it just was easier to build a wall around those places. I felt that because my daughter had lived, I should not be having such intense waves of grief and recurring trauma. Surely people have been in far worse situations, with far worse outcomes. I felt pangs of guilt for being so emotionally and spiritually distraught when we had experienced a good outcome.

Around the same time that God impressed upon me to write this book, He gave me a vision of myself in a flashback to a time shortly after the incident—maybe a few days afterward. I was in the shower, on my hands and knees under the water, and I was crying out to God, "Who am I that You would do that for ME? I am not worthy of Your grace. Was that You? Why?" This scene played out like a movie before my eyes, and I heard a whisper: *"I AM. I am worthy, and I bought you with My blood. Don't you know who you are? You were made for such a time as this."* This was two years after "the thing," where God showed me that vision. This was the most wonderful experience after such a long time of grief, strife, and pain. I had done a lot of damage to my relationships. I had retreated and pulled back from those who loved me, and I felt like no one could possibly understand what I was going through. I wanted to die, but I hid that from the closest people in my life, and I was unable to allow anyone near that dark reality. I built such strong walls around me, thinking I was protecting myself, but what I was really doing was responding to the wrong message. I believed the lies of the enemy. Reflecting on this, I often wonder how many times God tried telling me that but I was not willing to hear it.

It was helpful to talk to a neutral party in counseling to help me process my feelings and to get helpful tools to utilize once an attack started to happen. Anyone who has ever dealt with trauma, depression, or anxiety can attest that the feelings they are having make them feel "out of control." I am not suggesting refusing professional help here. I did all of those things through this process, and I found value through each step and connection I made in the professional setting. I went to counseling and did EMDR therapy, but it was not until I studied *who I was* and *whose I was* that the battle of the mind was won…once and for all—supernaturally. Once I started seeking God for more specific answers in prayer in the context of a relationship, most of the time out of despair, God started showing me and speaking life over me in a way I had never experienced before.

In the following chapters, I am going to show you what your identity is as a child of God, what that means, and the authority that it gives you over all power of the enemy. I will show you how to decree and declare the Word of the Lord over your life. This was my assignment and the intention that has been given to me by the Lord.

If you do not personally have an intimate relationship with God, but you believe He is your Lord, can we pause and seek Him on your behalf? I invite you to reflect on areas in your life where trauma has occurred and ask God, "Where were You?" Invite Him to speak to you, and ask Him to reveal the lie that you have believed about that situation. He wants to be your Friend, your Savior, the Person to whom you run and with whom you walk. He is our Companion and Helper, and He does send help. He will show you how much He loves you.

If you have gotten this far into my story and you are currently not walking with the Lord but you desire that for yourself and you believe that apart from Him you can do nothing, that He came to die for your sins and that He wants to walk with you on this journey, I encourage you to say a simple prayer to declare Him as your Lord and Savior and invite Him into your heart. You will not regret it. He is the best Friend anyone could ever dream of. He loves you without measure, and He wants more for you than your wildest dreams.

Satan knows there are generations out there that are spiritually subdued. He has worked his way into church circles to make people believe that God does not move today. We are numb, walking around this world just going through the motions. Our calendars are overwhelming, and the joy in our lives is lacking. It is time to begin to understand the mighty warrior that you are and at last defeat a powerless enemy.

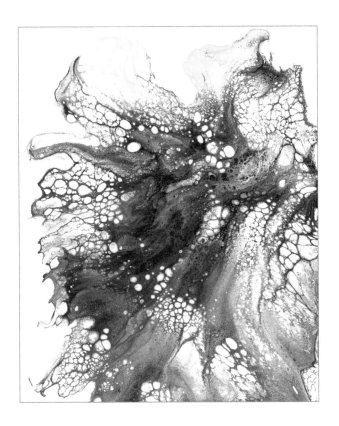

DON'T YOU KNOW WHO YOU ARE?

The greatest threat to Satan is when the people of God realize their identity in the One who created them. Knowing who God is, is knowing who you are. This freedom is free to all those who believe that they are sinners and believe that Jesus, God's Son, came to earth to die for their sins. The enemy of God's primary mission is to get people to turn away from Jesus and abandon the commission that was given to us by Jesus. What was this commission? To spread the good news of what Jesus has done. Romans 12:2 says: *"Do not be conformed to this world, but be transformed by the renewal of your mind, that by testing you may discern what is the will of God, what is good and acceptable and perfect*" (esv). Satan spends a significant amount of time to keep you away from discerning what is of this world and what is of God. He uses past hurts, past mistakes, temptations, accusations, pain, wounds, circumstances, and twisted or half truths as a way to derail you from receiving the promises of God. The tactics of the enemy are primarily targeted to individuals who say that they are followers of Jesus, because if he can keep you from your identity and the will of God on your life, then you are not a threat to his mission. I would also like to go so far as to say that he will ramp up his efforts of attack on those who are in the process of realizing the authority that they hold. To those who are not complacent. To those who have a God-given mission. To those that are right on the verge of breakthrough. Satan would not attack and increase those fiery arrows (Ps. 76:4) if he did not know who you actually were and how close you were. Not being rooted and grounded in the Word of God leaves a direct line of deception regarding your identity in Christ. If you are not renewing your mind in these concepts daily, you are building your identity on something false, and when that identity is tested, it will be shaken, and inevitably fall. When you renew your mind to what God says over you, hearing the opposite will make you pause. You will begin to recognize what the truth really is, but it takes practice. Daily appliance of the armor of God is required because the spiritual warfare against your mind is very real. When God asked me, *"Don't you know who you are?"* I truly did not have an answer. My response was, "I suppose not," and "I had better find out." True identity occurs when you realize who God says you are, and your destiny is established when you figure out what you were placed on this earth to do in His name. This is by no means an exhaustive list, but meditating and soaking in these three truths about who you are will have a big impact in your healing, deliverance, and wholeness.

Who Is God?

What a powerful and daunting question. How can a person effectively describe the Creator of all things, who is infinite in ALL things? Throughout history, people have attempted to define the nature of God. He is far greater than our minds can even imagine and more than I can even begin to write. I will give you a sampling of who He is to me—and even my attempt to do that somehow seems like an impossible task. We try to put God in a box to fit our theology or our present circumstances or ideals, but that is not how God works. He is all-knowing, and we yield to His movement, not vice versa. Despite all our attempts at controlling situations, circumstances, and our lives in general, He is so lovingly merciful and patient toward us. I often wonder if God, Jesus, and the Holy Spirit watch us and ponder at our struggles to define everything, knowing full well what the outcome will be.

We know that He is the same yesterday, today, and forever (Heb. 13:8). He is creative (Gen. 1:1), and He wants to collaborate with us in creating works for His kingdom (Exod. 35:35). He is the beginning and the end, the first and the last (Rev. 22:13). He knows everything. He knows your every thought; He knows your future, and nothing can be hidden from Him (Luke 12:2). He is always near, whether you know or recognize it (John 14:18). He sent His Son, who was fully God and fully man, to take the punishment of our transgressions. He has sent a Helper, a Comforter, His Spirit to dwell within us (1 John 4:13). He is the Lord who heals. In Psalm 30:2, the writer declares: *"Lord my God, I cried to you for help, and you healed me"* (niv). I have experienced many instances of the healing power of the Lord—emotionally, physically, and spiritually. He is most powerful, strong, and mighty, known to destroy and terrify the enemy, and we are protected by this (Rev. 15:3). He is the God of miracles, signs, and wonders. Nothing is impossible for Him. He is a mountain-moving God, and He has given us authority, powered by faith to speak to a mountain and move it (Mark 11:23). This might mean a physical mountain, but I believe that most of the time, this means that when we are faced with hard circumstances or unfathomable occurrences, even emotional thoughts or feelings that counter what God says about us, He said that if there is even a sliver of faith in you—then you can speak to it and it will move. Speak to depression, panic, anxiety, shame, or whatever is standing in your way, boldly confront it, and say MOVE! God promises that it shall be moved. He is the mighty Provider (Gen. 22:14), and everything that we need He will provide. He is a good Father, and if you are a parent, you understand the desire to give your children good gifts. In Matthew 7:11, Jesus explains how good our heavenly Father is to us. Even for we sinful people who can't do good enough to receive salvation, our good heavenly Father gave us Jesus to pay the price so that our salvation would be free. It doesn't stop there, however. He wants to give us the desires of our hearts (Ps. 37:4) on a much grander scale than we even desire for our own children. Those areas that look extreme or impossible gives God an opportunity. He loves to show off for you and through you; will you give Him your yes? He sent His only Son to save humanity (John 3:16). He is the kindest person I have ever encountered. His loving-kindness will be there to meet you in your darkest hour, regardless of what you have done. There is no condemnation. He is patient, He is kind, He is merciful, and He is fierce. This does not even scratch the surface of who the Almighty is. It is just a sampling to help you see who He wants to be for you, too. It is important for us to remind ourselves of who He is, because it is in Him that we fully understand who we are.

Who are you?

Again, it is impossible for me to cover all the areas of who you are in Christ Jesus—your identity. I am going to begin by giving you three foundational concepts. Let this take root as you ponder these concepts and allow the Holy Spirit to expand these for you. Receive these, because God created YOU as unique and He needs you to understand this so He can give you even greater things.

You were created in God's image.

So God created mankind in his own image, in the image of God he created them; male and female he created them.

—Genesis 1:27 NIV

This concept is so grand, abstract, and unimaginable to some. God moves beyond our human logical thought and thinking. God-type thoughts extend beyond our time and space parameters, and they tend to inspire more questions as we ponder more deeply. It is like when my daughter asks, "But who created God?" It is just so abstract for our minds to conceive that *no one* created God and that all things through Him are possible. Humanity was created as superior to all other beings, and we were made with a spirit and a soul in God's image. Why? To reflect His nature, to think His thoughts, to have dominion over the earth, to bring glory to God.

When Adam disobeyed the command from God in Genesis 3 and ate the forbidden fruit from the tree of the knowledge of good and evil, humankind experienced separation from God, loss of eternal life, disruption in relationships, and eventual physical death. How did Satan accomplish this? He made Eve question the voice of God and then used Eve to negatively influence Adam. They were walking with God in person, in a very intimate relationship with the Creator, and they were still deceived by Satan. He caused them to question, "Did God really say that?" If Satan can get us to question the voice of God and our ability to hear Him, it makes it more difficult to be a confident child of God. We were made to hear the voice of God, and yet, doubt has filled our culture. Jesus came to restore that covenant. He paid for the sins of this fallen world when He died on the cross.

We are instructed over one hundred times in the Bible to "fear nothing." Fear is completely covered by the blood of Jesus, and when we draw closer to Him, we can gain more wisdom and insight into the things that worry us. When babies are born, they are completely dependent on their caregivers for food, care, and safety. It is similar from a spiritual aspect. Our relationship with God—growing in that relationship, growing in wisdom, having communion and dialogue with God—is a nurtured process. I would not be telling you the truth if I said I have never worried a day in my life after beginning my relationship with Jesus. I still get crippling anxiety that sometimes takes my breath away, but I can now recognize those first signs of it and know it is not of God or from God. I can take those worries to the most kind, loving, gentle, and fierce One and lay them at His feet. When I do this, I gain more understanding or insight into a problem, or I completely let it go out of my hands.

When I start to feel crippling anxiety, it also gives me pause, and I say to myself, *What lie am I believing right now? Lord, where are You right now, and what do You want to say to me?*" He is a good Father, and He wants to have a relationship with you. He already knows what ails you, but He wants you to talk to Him about it, and He will break the chains of the attack off of you in an instant.

When I was growing up, the passive concept that "If it is God's will, then He will do it," had gained popularity. Friends, let me just interject here and tell you it *absolutely is God's will* for you to be *completely restored* in mind, body, and spirit. God is waiting for you to make a move. He has already willed it, but we must act! We must step out in faith and take action!

One powerful way to start waking up your mind to the fact that you are created in God's image is to make declarations to God. I will cover declarations and decrees in another chapter, but for now, make this declaration right now over your life:

- *I declare that I was created in God's image.*

- *I declare that I am a child of God, and I am deeply loved.*

- *I declare that God is working all things for my good.*

- *I declare that what the enemy meant for evil, God will use for good in my life.*

You are chosen.

For we know, brothers and sisters loved by God, that he has chosen you.

—*1 Thessalonians 1:4 NIV*

"For many are called, but few are chosen."

—*Matthew 22:14 NLT*

What does it mean that "many are called, but few are chosen," as it says in Matthew 22:14? I have spent a significant time wrestling with this idea, because I have often wondered, *What if I missed God? What if I blew it? What if I lost my spiritual inheritance?* Friends, we are not that powerful to be able to hinder God's will and plans for us—but we *do* have the ability to turn it away. What this verse says to me is that God has given sainthood to each of us. Each of us has an invitation to be a co-heir with Christ and have an inheritance, but He also gave us free will. We have the opportunity to choose Him and to say yes to all that is offered to us, just as we have a free will to say no and decline all that is offered. Matthew 22:14 means that He has opened His arms open wide to all of His people, but few will choose Him in return.

When I finally understood this, the fear of the Lord fell on me hard. I want to always choose Him and Him alone, but it is a continual process. Satan wants to knock us off track and hinder us from completing our kingdom missions. This is the sole reason I have continued to press on and finish this book despite all that has come against me to give up on this project—because you may be a woman reading this right now who is at such a low point in life that you have begun to believe the lie that there is nothing more for you in this life. Alternatively, you may be a woman who is believing the false narrative that you can do all things yourself, that you do not need anyone. This is a direct attack and a lie from the enemy; above everything else, Satan wants to alter the path of women and take them out of the will of God for their lives. Genesis 3:15 tells us of the lifetime antagonistic relationship that continues between women and Satan: *"And I will cause hostility between you and the woman, and between your offspring and her offspring. He will strike your head, and you will strike his heel"* (niv). It is also written in Revelation 12:17: *"And the dragon was enraged at the woman, and went to make war with the rest of her children, who keep the commandments of God and hold to the testimony of Jesus. And the dragon stood on the sand of the seashore"* (nasb). Ladies, may your heels be permanently bruised from stomping Satan's head!

Satan hates you, and he will stop at nothing until you believe the lie that God does not love you or that He does not care. We are at war. You cannot truly wage the war to win until you know who you are and what your identity is in Christ. If you do not own your identity, what authority do you have?

Satan laughed in my face for many years because I did not know my identity. He absolutely knows the plans God has for me, and it terrifies and angers him, but I am not a threat to him if I do not walk in my identity and authority. The bigger the threat you are to the enemy, the more he will intensify the attacks against you. His tactics are very predictable. Satan is not creative; he does not have the ability to create anything, only pervert what has already been created. His tactics are always to steal, kill, deceive, destroy, and dethrone you—yes, *dethrone* you. Ephesians 2:6 states, *"And God raised us up with Christ and seated us with him in the heavenly realms in Christ Jesus"* (niv). If you are a co-heir with Christ, and you are seated in heavenly places at the same time as you walk this earth, you are royalty, and Satan's mission is to dethrone you.

If you are currently walking through a hard time, when it feels like you are down and repeatedly being kicked, when things just do not seem to go your way, keep pressing on. Victory is closer than you could ever know. Do not allow the enemy to create fear in you about his power on this earth. You were given authority over all of Satan's power, but you have to claim that authority through your identity.

The refreshing thing about all of this is that God wants to be near you far more than you desire to be near Him. He is never far from you, and a whisper from your heart will have Him rushing in at an instant. To destroy Satan in his tracks, you must be grounded in the Word of God. This is a fierce weapon at our disposal that God has given you to wage war against the enemy, which is your sword. God's Word is like a double-edged sword (Heb. 4:12). It has the ability to divide what is real and what is not and make known the intents of your heart and attitudes. God looks at the matters of the heart— our intentions and our motives—and His Word separates everything that is not of Him through His Word. Invite the Lord to search your heart today and test your anxious thoughts (Ps. 139:23). Through this process, allow His Word to sever the lies that you have held onto and allow Him to reveal the truth to your heart.

We must renew our minds each day with the living Word of God and apply the full armor of God, as listed in Ephesians 6 in order to take a stand against the devil's schemes. So, stand firm and apply the belt of truth around your waist—the core belief that God created us, that He speaks to us, that He sent Jesus to save us, and that we have been given the Holy Spirit as our Helper. This belt protects your will and guards you against temptation. You can always refer to the truth, which separates the ways of this world from the ways of God. The belt of truth secures your breastplate of righteousness in place. The breastplate covers your vital organs and keeps them from harm; you are protected. Spiritually, you were forgiven as a sinner and accepted by the loving Father. This was not due to self-righteousness, but through faith we are found in Him and we have His righteousness. Plant your feet and stand on the gospel of peace, proclaiming the Good News of salvation and peace everywhere you go, always available and ready. (Remember the Great Commission?) The devil wants you to believe that telling people about the freedom they can have in Christ is worthless and hopeless, but it is our main delegation in this life and it is a joy and an honor to do so.

Supplementary to these items, we have been given other aspects of the armor that can be used in defense or as offensive weapons. We must take up the shield of faith, which furnishes us with protection from the attacks of the enemy in the form of insults and setbacks. We must shield ourselves by refusing to believe those lies. God also shields us with His faithfulness. We are also to place a helmet of salvation on our heads. Helmets are key identifiers of who is actually in the army of God. Historically with combat armor, you could immediately identify who was on your side and who was on the other side by the markings or unique characteristics on the helmet. The helmet of salvation marks you as a saint, a co-heir with Christ. The helmet not only identifies you, but it also protects your mind from satanic attacks that cause you to doubt God. Finally, my favorite weapon is the sword of the Spirit, which is the living Word of God, the Bible. The Word protects you and brings absolute truth, which is a strong weapon against the lies of the enemy. God's Word is a double-edged sword that will separate all truth from lies and will bring revelation to those with eyes to see and ears to hear. The Word is our surefire way to defeat the attacks of the enemy in our lives.

You are fearfully and wonderfully made.

I praise you because I am fearfully and wonderfully made; your works are wonderful, I know that full well.

— *PSALM 139:14 NASB*

What does it mean to be fearfully and wonderfully made? My first identity point was that we are made in God's image. This point, that we are fearfully and wonderfully made, is intimately connected to that point. It drives home that message, but it also signifies something that most people miss when they read this passage. We did not just appear out of thin air. We did not evolve from the form of an animal. We were not even created by our parents. We did not create ourselves. God, the Creator of all things, thought of each one of us and crafted us in the likeness of Himself. We were made to adore and worship our Creator and to have the fear of the Lord as part of our innermost being. The fear of the Lord does not mean that we are fearful of God and His presence out of terror; it actually is the opposite. To fear the Lord, or to have the Spirit of the fear of the Lord, is to fear His absence in our lives, or to be far away from Him or His will upon our lives. The consequence of the absence of God is eternal damnation in hell and to experience the wrath of God. This is of the upmost importance to understand who you are as a child of God and where you will spend eternity.

Not understanding this point can be devastating to your identity because Satan wants you to believe that you can do all things…by yourself. Satan whispers to us: *You are the manifesto of your wildest dreams. If you set your sights on something, if you work hard enough, if you have enough will—then it will be given to you. If you just put it out in the "universe," then the stars will align for you and give you what you want.*

Your very breath, your existence, your success, your desires, your dreams should reflect the kingdom of God. Why? Because YOU were fearfully and wonderfully made in the image of the Creator.

The Bible says in 2 Corinthians 3:18: *"And we all, with unveiled face, beholding the glory of the Lord, are being transformed into the same image from one degree of glory to another. For this comes from the Lord who is the Spirit"* (nasb). When you look in the mirror, if you know your identity, who you are in Christ Jesus, and if you believe that you have been created for kingdom impact, and if the veil has been lifted—meaning you have accepted Christ as your Savior—then you should see Jesus there in the mirror, because He is at work in you.

This happened to me recently when I caught my reflection in the mirror. On the exterior, I looked like a mess—I had not showered, my hair was up in a messy bun, and I was still wearing my pajamas. I caught my reflection as I walked by the mirror, and it astounded me. I was not experiencing vanity; I was not seeing external beauty according to the standards set by society, but I saw Jesus in me, and His glory was shining through. The beauty I saw was not of me, but it was what was in me that made me raise my hands and praise the Father, who has promised that we would be the light of the world.

For you formed my inward parts; you knitted me together in my mother's womb. I praise you, for I am fearfully and wonderfully made. Wonderful are your works; my soul knows it very well. My frame was not hidden from you, when I was being made in secret, intricately woven in the depths of the earth. Your eyes saw my unformed substance; in your book were written, every one of them, the days that were formed for me, when as yet there was none of them.

— *Psalm 139:13–16 esv*

Have you ever thought about the human body and all the intricate details that must function simultaneously just for you to take a breath? I think about these things often, because that is my background as a nurse. I am often in awe of God for His handiwork in the human body. While working in health care, when I would see the breakdown of body parts and systems of the body, it baffled me—because it is a miracle that *more does not go wrong* with us on a daily basis.

So much grace is given to these bodies in which we live. For as much damage we intentionally and unintentionally do to ourselves by not eating right, not exercising, not getting rest, and stressing about each and every thing, and being constantly bombarded with environmental poisons it still takes quite a bit to cause a disease process. Then, many people live with an ailment for a significant amount of time before it becomes a threat to their lives.

Besides the intricate work that goes on at a cellular level and the different body systems working both independently and simultaneously together, God gave us a mind, emotions, and thoughts—or our soul and the ability to think for ourselves, to form thoughts and opinions. Our physical bodies respond to known and unknown chemical signals that are created from our thoughts or feelings. From a purely physical aspect, if you put your hand over a candle flame, a signal will travel to the brain subconsciously and tell your hand to move, and your body will respond. Am I the only one who marvels at this?

If you are suffering from PTSD, like I was, your body is living in what we call a sustained sympathetic response, or fight or flight. You can be triggered by a threat or stimulus that comes at you unexpectedly; for me it was loud noises or being touched without being prepared for it. Subconsciously, your body prepares to either fight to protect itself or to run away. Physical symptoms on a cellular level include an increased blood flow to the periphery of your body (your arms and legs) so that it can take action. The blood vessels constrict to increase blood pressure and increase your heart rate so that your body has an adequate amount of blood and oxygen needed to save your life.

This is not a healthy state in which to live for extended periods of time. It is impossible to rest or have a fully healthy and functioning digestive system when you are constantly living in a sympathetic state. Rational thought processes are also impossible. If you have experienced this, you know that what people say to you when you are in this state is not adequately processed, received, or used logically.

The hands of God formed you with exquisite and intricate detail. He knows the number of hairs on your head (Matt. 10:30). He cares about every detail about your life because He created you. You have been fearfully and wonderfully made in the likeness of Christ to do mighty works—works that will blow your mind. Submit to Him and let Him tell you all the ways He loves you. When I pray with my kids at night, I always pray this: "Holy Spirit, hover over these kids as they sleep and whisper in their ears everything You hold dear about each of them." Friend, I pray that over you right now. I pray that the Holy Spirit, who hovered over the deep and breathed life into existence, will hover over you at night and whisper in your ear everything He loves about you. I pray that He teaches you how to lean into Him, to separate what is of Him and what is not, in Jesus' mighty name, amen!

ALL THAT CAN BE SHAKEN (AND GREAT WAS ITS FALL)

"Therefore everyone who hears these words of Mine and acts on them, may be compared to a wise man who built his house on the rock. And the rain fell, and the floods came, and the winds blew and slammed against that house; and yet it did not fall, for it had been founded on the rock. Everyone who hears these words of Mine and does not act on them, will be like a foolish man who built his house on the sand. The rain fell, and the floods came, and the winds blew and slammed against that house; and it fell—and great was its fall."

—MATTHEW 7:24–27 NASB, EMPHASIS MINE

"Everyone who hears these words of Mine and does not act on them..." Friends, Jesus is not talking about unbelievers here. He is talking about people who have professed that Jesus is their Lord and who call themselves followers of Christ. Only people who know Him have "ears to hear" Him. They have ears to hear—and yet they do nothing. They live for this world and the comforts to which we have grown accustomed.

This would include each one of us if we do not wake up and not only be hearers but be doers of the Word. James 1:22 says, *"Do not merely listen to the word, and so deceive yourselves. Do what it says"* (niv). This is how we bring heaven to earth. This is how each of us can build the kingdom, even if we are not ministers, theologians, or Bible scholars. This is how we impact our workplaces: We love the Lord our God with all our heart, and we love our neighbor as ourselves (Matt. 22:37–39).

There is so much power in the statement "and *yet*" as it reads in Matthew 7:25 (nasb): *And yet*, for everyone who hears these words and *acts* on them will see results. There are many believers of Christ and professing Christians who are complacent—and this is what the enemy wants. However, for those who have ears to hear and have the wisdom to understand, in order to withstand the shaking in this world, we must not only hear the Word, but we must act.

Proverbs 9:10 states, *"The fear of the Lord is the beginning of wisdom, and knowledge of the Holy One is understanding"* (esv). Wisdom begins from fearing the absence of the Lord and beholding His never ending power. You begin to understand when you start to know Him through relationship, through the renewing of your mind, through contentment, through not conforming to this world, through being in communion, and through love. This gives you a solid foundation—a rock—on which to stand and to build, because the rain is going to fall. The hardships of life have come and will continue to come. Heartache is inevitable and tragedies will happen, but if your foundation is solid, your house will not fall because it was built upon the wisdom and knowledge of God.

It should be no surprise when you take a brief assessment of the world in which we currently live, that things seem shaky and a little unstable. Does it feel at times that the world could implode at any given moment? It is volatile, unstable, and ready to react at a given notice. Things are shaking. I encourage you to evaluate where your foundation has been built upon. Is it on the rock—the written Word of God? Or on the sand—the culture and what the world is doing and saying?

If you are not grounded and rooted in the foundations of Christ, including what God says about you, you are at risk for a fall. As Matthew 7:27 says, "*And it fell—and great was its fall*" (nasb). I know this from experience. In the midst of my own turmoil and trauma, I was not clinging to God. I allowed myself to be filled with hopelessness. I gave room for Satan to have his way, to steal, kill, and destroy everything around me. The solid foundation upon which I thought I rested turned out to be built on sand, not merely because I did not love God—I absolutely did—but because of a lack of intimacy in our relationship. It was like a relationship with someone whom I saw as a personal hero. God was like someone I was familiar with: I knew what He was about, I was aware of His presence with others, the good works that He had done, and I was a huge fan, but I did not understand what it meant to host the presence of God in my life, to die to myself, carry my cross, and be filled with the Holy Spirit. When the trauma of almost losing my child occurred, the presence of the Lord appeared, and all that could be shaken was shaken.

I grew up in the church; in fact, I come from a family of pastors. I gave my life to Christ when I was seven, and I continued to attend church as I grew up. I would often be worried every time I went to church that I just could not quite measure up to God in order to be truly saved. I never understood what it meant to bring God my cares and concerns because I always felt like I needed to "fix" myself before I could come to Him. It also felt impossible to get to a point where I was good enough for Him. The pillars of my faith had been built on shaky ground. I knew *of* God, but I did not *personally* know Him.

Progressing through young adulthood is an interesting and difficult time for everyone. I felt so unprepared for life on my own when I got to college. My life felt like it was simultaneously in fast-forward and in slow motion. Does that make sense? When I reflect on that time in my life, that is exactly how I see it—in fast-forward *and* in slow motion, at the very same time. I felt so lost and small in a big, fast-moving world that I was sure I was missing something. Interestingly, I had many friends who actually told me I always seemed so put together, as if I had things figured out. I do not know how I was able to portray one reality on the outside while living another reality on the inside, but that is how so many of us have been navigating this life.

Social media portrays a constant stream of perfect life moments while hiding the darker moments, a direct outward experience that I faced twenty years ago. Even though I had been raised in the church, I did not know I could take my brokenness to God. I had never been taught about my identity, or told that I could submit my hardest heart, the fortress around my mind and emotions, and the lies that I believed about myself and God, and that He could penetrate and dismantle all of it in an instant. Instead, I continued to build a strong exterior that appeared put together, but on the inside I was scared, unsure, self-conscious, bitter, and angry. And when turmoil eventually came upon me and shook my foundation, what remained was a broken person whose identity had been built on falsities and who had become exposed to the world.

What became my outward manifestations during that time were the interior bricks that was holding the house up in the form of insecurities, bitterness, and anger. I believe that God knew these circumstances were going to be the perfect time to build a foundation of character—and build it upon the rock. He covered me with His pinions, and under His wings He allowed me to seek refuge. He was a faithful shield for me as I took on a new form and became a new creation in Him through this process (Ps. 91:4). He surrounded me with strong and mature people of faith who continued to help and guide me—and above all, love me. Even though it did not feel comfortable at the time, when I reflect on these moments, I see Him everywhere around me.

While you were reading about my experiences, did it bring to mind any areas in your life in which you feel the foundation of your identity was built upon shaky ground? It is okay to be vulnerable to God with your thoughts about this. He already knows who you are and what areas are weak in you. God wants to give you more. He has massive plans for your life, and He desires for you to fulfill them in order to fulfill His own mandate to bring heaven to earth. He does not need any of us to fulfill anything, but He created us to be in partnership, relationship, and to co-labor with Him. He cannot give you more if your foundation cannot bear the weight of it. He is so merciful not to give you more than what you can carry. That does not mean that He will not stretch you in order to build your faith and seek Him, but that means that He will not give you a bigger assignment if you have not done the work to build up your foundation and make it solid. Your faith will stand the tests that come at you, and your character will become more reflective of Jesus.

None of this means we are perfect. The Bible clearly states that we are not and will not be free from the snares of this world until the return of Christ Jesus. But His promises are new each morning, and we can continually come to Him and keep trying. He is so patient with us. No matter how many times we fail the test, He will encourage us to keep trying again.

I encourage you to list three areas of your life below in which you have partnered with a lie and on which you would like God to give you more clarity. Writing them down, and not just thinking about them, allows them to take form and give you a visual. Speaking them out loud, as in a conversation with God, allows Him the space necessary to speak back to you.

If you feel comfortable, I invite you to do so now in the area provided below. Just take a moment before proceeding to sit and allow God to speak to you. You might get a picture, you might think of a word that pops up in your mind, or you might feel an emotion. Feel free to write down next to each item what you are sensing God is saying to you. This exercise is what we call an "activation," and it involves practicing hearing God for yourself. If you are unsure if a sensation was from you or from God, you can always test it against God's Word. I keep a Bible app on my phone so that no matter where I am, I can search the Scriptures while on the go. God will never contradict His Word, so if what you are hearing is counter to what the Bible says, then I encourage you to take that thought captive and speak to it out loud that it must go. This is practicing your authority in Jesus. Keep going through this exercise until you feel confident that it was God speaking to you. Then I encourage you to begin to pray what He has spoken over you; make it a declaration and decree it in Jesus' name.

Prayer

Father, I come to You now and lift all Your sons and daughters up at this time who are reading this book and are struggling with their identity in You. Allow Your Word to cut through any lie that was spoken over them about their identity, the promises You have made to them, and the plans that You have for them. I speak to the items that they wrote down, Lord, and I ask that You give them clarity and the answers they are seeking. For the sake of Your daughters, Lord, give them the strength to see Your image in their reflections and to strike the enemy with their declarations. Make it apparent to them all areas where Satan has caused division and strife in their lives, right now in Jesus' name. Let them feel that they were made for a kingdom purpose, in Your image. Help them to understand that they were fearfully and wonderfully made and they are a direct threat to the kingdom of darkness. We seek You first, Lord. Thank You for Your grace and patience as we are awakened to Your never-ending promises. May our hearts be open and ready for You, Lord. In Your mighty name, amen and amen.

Declarations

- *I declare that the weakened areas of my foundation will be revealed and replaced by the truth of who God is.*

- *I declare that He hides me in His pinions, and under His wings I can seek refuge.*

- *I declare that He gives me a shield of His faithfulness and that I am completely hidden in Christ Jesus for full and complete restoration in Jesus' name.*

IDENTITY
TO AUTHORITY

Does it matter if you know your identity as a child of God? I am going to invite you on a tangent for a moment to address something that is on the Father's heart for His sons and daughters. In my time spent with the Lord praying over this project, I kept hearing: *"Teach them who they are."* As I started down this journey myself, I thought I *did* know who I was as a child of God. But God revealed my weakness in this area—and the reason why I was weak.

I cannot claim to have all the answers about this, but as I was instructed by the Lord, I am sharing my personal experience in learning more about Him. This, in turn, has revealed who I am. God then instructed me to teach and equip His daughters—that's you!—with the same revelatory knowledge so they could also stand firm in who He sees them, thus giving them the ability to walk, live, and breathe their authority and power. Until you know the authority you have, you will remain powerless against the enemy's attacks, and you cannot understand the authority you have until you know who you are.

Authority in Christ gives you power. Not walking in your given authority and power will cause you to walk upon this earth just going through the motions in a state of complacency, tossed in all directions by the storms that come at you, subject to worldly events, and succumbed by fear by the instability this world offers. The most dangerous place to be in the body of Christ is in a state of complacency. According to the *Merriam-Webster's Dictionary*, *complacency* is the state of simultaneously being self-assured or satisfied with something while also being unaware of danger. This stems from a spirit of pride, and it prevents a person from heeding warnings or thinking critically about a matter. People in this state lack discernment, especially in the church, and they do not test the spirits by spending time with the Lord on messages being taught (1 John 4:1). We must test the spirits behind what is spoken, not to condemn a teacher, but because Satan will stop at nothing, including infiltrating the church, to deceive the heirs of Christ. When we spend time with the Lord by further studying a teaching, we are inviting the Lord to reveal His heart to us. We do not test the Spirit to pick it apart, the ultimate goal is to learn how to hear from the Lord. It also opens up dialogue with your pastor if there is a point in the message that you are not understanding. As we communicate to understand the Word of God with other believers, we sharpen each other and are accountable to one another. The real danger in being complacent is being ill prepared for the attacks that come from the enemy when we least expect it. This is the aspect of your walk with the Lord that Satan will hit the hardest at in his efforts to derail your assignment. He does this because he knows that your words can have damaging and deadly effects on the kingdom of darkness. It is critical—now more than ever—to ask for discernment in all things.

Filled with the Holy Spirit

The Holy Spirit not only indicated to me that this book was for anyone who was dealing with trauma—believer or not—but He also impressed upon me that those in the body of Christ needed to learn their identity. Even those who are mature believers could get something out of learning their importance in the body of Christ and how to operate in a way that brings glory to Jesus. Why? I grew up in the church my whole life and I did not know my identity in Christ, so if that was true about me, then there are others—if even just one—who needs to hear this message.

Many people are raised to go to church every week, but they are not equipped for living a life filled with Christ in the everyday moments, or even how to effectively pray. We have prayer ministries where we submit our ails and problems, and we trust that they will be handled by those who are in a direct communication network to God. Of course, it is wonderful to pray for each other and join in agreement for the move and touch of God in each of our lives, but we are not teaching people how to effectively speak to God for themselves. The church welcomes talking about God and Jesus, but speaking, knowing, and welcoming the Spirit of the Lord into our daily lives, recognizing Him as a Person and an integral component of the Godhead, has not been taught or welcomed in its full capacity. Our identity in Christ is not fully understood without welcoming the complete Trinity. Theology and doctrine are important, but it is not enough. Encountering the Holy Spirit and being empowered to walk in freedom, learning how to cause the bowels of hell to quake just by opening your mouth, and actually becoming the manifested light of this world (and not just using the phrase as a metaphor) is not taught.

I do not condemn pastors here—the weight of what they carry is heavy, and the pressure has caused many of them to walk away from their assignments. If the church were teaching people how to mature and grow in their own faith and journey with the Lord, maybe the weight on pastors would lessen. The Holy Spirit is our Advocate and Teacher, and He wants to walk alongside us to remind us of everything He has spoken (John 14:26).

Without the Holy Spirit, theology and teaching is dead and ineffective. When you invite Jesus into your life as your Lord and Savior, you are saved, and many supernatural events occur even if you are not aware of it. The blood of Jesus redeems you from all your sins (Eph. 1:7), you become unified to Christ and the collective body as a child of God (Col. 1:13), your end destination becomes heaven (Isa. 64:6), and you are made into a new creation (2 Cor. 5:17), just to name a few. As an outward statement, a prophetic act of those supernatural occurrences, and a way to show your repentance and the washing away of your sins, you should participate in a water baptism. Your salvation does not hinge on water baptism, but this is an act of showing your faith, declaring your walk with the Lord, and cleansing yourself from sin. Salvation and the washing away of sins is required to receive the gift of the Holy Spirit according to apostle Paul: *"Each of you must repent of your sins and turn to God, and be baptized in the name of Jesus Christ for the forgiveness of your sins. Then you will receive the gift of the Holy Spirit. This promise is to you, to your children, and to those far away – all who have been called by the Lord our God."* (Acts 2:38 nlt).

John tells us in Luke 3:16 that there is more still to come. He writes, *"I baptize you with water; but he who is mightier than I is coming, the thong of whose sandals I am not worthy to untie; he will baptize you with the Holy Spirit and with fire"* (niv). During a water baptism, our sins are washed away, we are made new, and we are adopted into the one body as an outward statement of what took place when we welcomed Christ to reside in us. First Corinthians 12:13 describes our unification into one body and states, *"For we were all baptized by one Spirit so as to form one body—whether Jews or Gentiles, slave or free—and we were all given the one Spirit to drink"* (niv). And 1 Peter 3:21 describes the water baptism symbolizing the forgiveness of our sins through the resurrection power of Jesus, *"And this water symbolizes baptism that now saves you also—not the removal of dirt from the body but the pledge of a clear conscience toward God. It saves you by the resurrection of Jesus Christ."*

We can participate in a water baptism as a prophetic act and a statement that symbolizes Jesus' death on the cross and His resurrection. As we are submerged under the water, our old ways die on the cross with Jesus, and just as He was resurrected, as we emerge from the water, we are also resurrected a new being in Christ in an outward showing of the supernatural events that took place when we accepted Christ as our Lord.

I love the act of water baptism; in fact I have been baptized twice. The first time I was baptized was when I was seven years old, and the second time was when the Lord rescued me and revealed Himself to me through the trauma I had gone through. Baptism is a step of faith, and when I was redeemed from the trauma that I had experienced, I wanted to shout from the rooftops all that God had done for me. I do want to switch and focus more on a more controversial topic in the church, which is the baptism of the Holy Spirit. I know there are many schools of thought on this, and this topic has caused many arguments and divisions among church circles and denominations throughout history. I encourage you to stick with me through this and open your heart to receive what the Lord placed on my heart. Many books have been written on the Holy Spirit, about how He operates, and there are many far more qualified than I to discuss this, but I am going to share my personal experience, what I have witnessed of the Holy Spirit, and reference my understanding of it from the Bible.

As a disclaimer, anytime someone breaks down and delves into areas of the Bible for understanding, I encourage you to take it as an invitation to dive in deeper for yourself. Do not take my words at face value; seek for yourself and allow the Holy Spirit to speak to you through His Word.

The Gospels tell the story of the witnessed baptism of the Holy Spirit upon Jesus at the same time He was baptized in water:

Then Jesus came from Galilee to the Jordan to be baptized by John. But John tried to deter him, saying, "I need to be baptized by you, and do you come to me?" Jesus replied, "Let it be so now; it is proper for us to do this to fulfill all righteousness." Then John consented. As soon as Jesus was baptized, he went up out of the water. At that moment heaven was opened, and he saw the Spirit of God descending like a dove and alighting on him. And a voice from heaven said, "This is my Son, whom I love; with him I am well pleased."

—*MATTHEW 3:13–17 NIV*

Once Jesus was baptized with the Holy Spirit, His ministry began, and He was equipped and clothed in power to fulfill His mission. Some believe that the water baptism and the Holy Spirit baptism occur at the same time, this was how I was taught my entire upbringing. While it did for Jesus, it didn't for others who were receiving water baptisms at that time—because Jesus was still with them. The Holy Spirit would come to be with them after Jesus ascended into heaven. After Jesus was crucified and then rose from the dead, He remained with His disciples for forty days so that He could teach them what was to come and the ways of the Kingdom. They would then proclaim it to the world and equip others to do the same. Jesus told them to wait—even after they had been with Him in ministry for three years and were instructed one on one by Him for forty days following the resurrection. They were not yet ready for their ministry because they needed *power*. That power was to come to them by the Holy Spirit and they were not to proceed until that occurred.

Before Jesus went up to heaven, He said this: *"For John baptized you in water, but in a few days from now you will be baptized in the Holy Spirit!"* (Acts 1:5 tpt). In order to fulfill the mandate that Jesus was giving them, they needed to be filled with the Holy Spirit, not for their own salvation-they were saved through their belief in Jesus and their relationship with Him, but to have the power to complete their assignment. It goes on to say this in the following chapter:

On the day Pentecost was being fulfilled, all the disciples were gathered in one place. Suddenly they heard the sound of a violent blast of wind rushing into the house from out of the heavenly realm. The roar of the wind was so overpowering it was all anyone could bear! Then all at once a pillar of fire appeared before their eyes. It separated into tongues of fire that engulfed each one of them. They were all filled and equipped with the Holy Spirit and were inspired to speak in tongues—empowered by the Spirit to speak in languages they had never learned!

—ACTS 2:1–5 TPT

My interpretation of this is that they were filled with the Holy Spirit with fire (power) to be equipped to do something, and they were given supernatural tools to be able to know what God was saying and to fulfill the mandate they were given. The apostle Peter tells us that his interpretation of the filling of the Holy Spirit on Pentecost was actually a fulfillment of prophecy by the prophet Joel: *"'In the last days,' God says, 'I will pour out my Spirit upon all people. Your sons and daughters will prophesy. Your young men will dream dreams. In those days I will pour out my Spirit even on my servants— men and woman alike— and they will prophesy'"* (Acts 2:16–18 nlt).

That continues to stand today. If it was considered "the last days" after Jesus ascended into heaven and we are still here on this earth some two thousand years later, we are most definitely still in "the last days." The Lord is still pouring out His Spirit upon people and as the Scripture says, it is meant for them to do something—to prophesy. We are all to earnestly desire spiritual gifts, especially that we would prophesy (1 Cor. 14:1). This is a direct invitation to partner with the Holy Spirit and welcome Him to work through us and with us.

In my opinion, being filled with the Holy Spirit, or being baptized with the Holy Spirit, is different from being born again or even being water-baptized by the Holy Spirit. Let me explain. You are given salvation through your belief in Jesus dying for your iniquities on the cross, He rose from the dead three days later, and He ascended into heaven. You are washed clean *by* the Holy Spirit through a water baptism, but you are baptized *with* the Holy Spirit when you are clothed in His presence, and there is a supernatural power that comes upon you to fulfill a kingdom mandate. It tells us in 1 Corinthians 4:20, *"For the kingdom realm of God comes with* power, *not simply impressive words"* (tpt, emphasis mine).

When you accept Christ as your Savior, the Spirit unites all believers as one body; you become a fellow heir and receive eternal life.

Accepting Christ, being water-baptized by the Holy Spirit, and being baptized with the Holy Spirit—all of these occurring at separate times has been my experience, despite being taught and believing differently my whole life. Our walk with the Lord is a journey, and the growth that occurs through all of these phases requires a lot of maturity along the way.

Not that it cannot happen all at once. I have heard wonderful stories of that being the case, and I believe that we may see rapid accelerations in the body of Christ in the coming days to catch us up to be who we were created to be, since we have been lulled to sleep by complacency. However the Spirit of the Lord chooses to move in an individual or a collective body, we need to remain open to what He wants to do and stay free from offense. Offense opens a door for Satan to infiltrate God's people and do damage. God is so wonderful in how He works in each individual's life. He works in ways that we cannot put into a box. What He does for one person is not necessarily what happens for another.

I am not arguing about theology, that the baptism has to occur in the same way every time, or that the way I was raised to believe was wrong. I am simply stating my personal journey and everything I was raised to believe about it was not the way I received it. The greater message here is that the Holy Spirit has been eliminated from discussion in many churches today. Allowing the Holy Spirit to move at will grips the hearts of people and it can get messy and unpredictable and keeping services constrained to an hour does not give an open invitation for the Holy Spirit to move at will.

My interpretation of the way I received the different baptisms was this: I received the Spirit of the Lord to reside *in* me when I accepted Jesus as my Lord and Savior, and I was washed clean *by* the Spirit through water baptism, which was an outward declaration of my salvation in Christ. I died to myself, and I emerged as a new creation with the DNA of Jesus. It was a public decree that I made to declare that I was a child of God. The baptism *with* the Holy Spirit took place when the Holy Spirit came upon me like fire and clothed me with His presence (Luke 24:49). He equipped me and gave me the power I needed to do works for the kingdom (such as writing this book).

There was absolutely no question about my baptism with the Holy Spirit; it was a tangible experience that I will not ever forget. The manifestation of the baptism of the Holy Ghost might look and be experienced differently among individuals, but no matter how it occurs for you – it will be unmistakable. For myself, there was a physical whole-body experience that actually felt like fire going through my entire body, and there was an encounter with the Lord that forever changed my life. The kind of empowerment that we receive in the baptism of the Holy Spirit might look different for each person and I believe that it can happen again and again. Why would we limit God to just one encounter with us when we converted into a new being when the Bible is very clear that He desires a close intimate walk with us? If there is that kind of experience available to all, why are we not desperately seeking it as a collective body of Christ? I believe a day is coming when we will be walking out an Acts kind of power that will be filled with supernatural miracles, signs, and wonders with no boundaries of faith denominations, but there must be a shaking in the body of Christ to be open and welcoming that kind of empowerment.

The Spirit of the Lord living inside you is for your personal salvation, journey, walk, and benefit with the Lord, but when the Holy Spirit comes upon you, you are granted power that is not yours; it is for the benefit of others. It gives you the means (it equips you) to do the work of the Lord, to make disciples of all nations, to heal the sick, to raise the dead, to perform signs, wonders, and miracles. This is not for your sake or for attention to be placed upon you, but it is to be done in the name of Jesus, for all the glory and honor to be His alone. This is so others can feel His love and be touched in ways they have never experienced before. All believers can receive this incredible gift, and this is how everyday people can impact cities, cultures, and nations.

Hindering the move of Holy Spirit and not equipping church members how to steward a relationship with Him, or even how to effectively pray, does a great disservice to the body of Christ. I believe this has been the devious work of Satan. When you understand your assignment, station, position, and authority in heavenly places, despite your station or position on the earth, your posture changes. You are given the ability to see circumstances differently, your reactions to offenses are different, and you see people through a different set of lenses. This is because our enemy is not flesh and blood, or people, but it is sin, principalities, forces of darkness, and Satan himself (Eph. 6:12). We should not fear this, but we must have a keen awareness and operate in discernment.

When you are given the power of the Holy Spirit, you are imparted with His gifts as He sees fit. The most common manifestations that are talked about in scripture include speaking in new tongues and prophesying (Acts 2:4, 18). That is but two gifts of the Holy Spirit that are mentioned in 1 Corinthians 12:8–10. The other seven include wisdom, knowledge, faith, healing, working of miracles, discerning of spirits, and interpretation of tongues. These gifts are given by one Spirit as the Spirit deems, and He knows no boundaries of denominations. Satan wants us to turn on each other and be a people divided. He knows what happens when the body of Christ is unified—it leads to his demise. When you walk in spiritual authority and divine love, that posture will slay everything that is not of God.

The church has become lukewarm and complacent and has turned away in cowardice from the attacks of the enemy so as not to offend others. The move of the Holy Spirit has become controversial and offensive—in the church! It has been marked as being "charismatic" and "weird." This is where discernment is so important in recognizing the Holy Spirit when He moves. Jesus' very existence was offensive. He offended people wherever He went—but He was only offensive to those who had hardened their hearts with religion and those whom the enemy had blinded. We must walk in our God-given authority through Jesus with love so that it is not our works, but His, that will shine through. That is where deliverance, salvation, and healing will take place. Barriers are broken, strongholds are brought down, principalities are demolished, and the people around us begin to feel the incredible love that God has for them, that they are seen by the Creator of all things. This all comes from the Holy Spirit, our Helper (John 14:16), our Advocate (John 14:16), the Spirit of glory (1 Pet. 4:14), the Spirit of prophecy (Rev. 19:10), the breath of the Almighty (Job 33:4), the oil of joy (Isa. 61:3), and so many other names that refer to Him throughout the Bible.

The identity as a son or daughter in Christ is free to everyone who believes that Jesus came to earth from heaven, fully man and fully God, and died for their sins, that He was raised from the dead three days later and now sits at the right hand of God, and that He has given us a Helper, the Holy Spirit, and will someday return in His second coming. John 3:16 states, *"For God so loved the world that he gave his one and only Son, that whoever believes in him shall not perish but have eternal life"* (niv). The church typically stops right there at that verse, but to behold the Gospel in its entirety we must also look to what happens in the end of days. It goes on to state in John 3:36: *"He who believes and trusts in the Son and accepts Him [as Savior] has eternal life [that is, already possesses it]; but he who does not believe the Son and chooses to reject Him, [disobeying Him and denying Him as Savior] will not see [eternal] life, but [instead] the wrath of God hangs over him continually"* (amp). We have to make the choice and know the consequences. Eternal life in heaven in perfect peace and harmony or eternal life of damnation and more pain than you could possibly bear. Eternal life in heaven is a comforting and amazing promise to comprehend—but there is more than just waiting for that day to arrive. The Lord is infinite in all His ways, and there is no way to comprehend fully what He has in store for us. He wants to build something with us, and He wants to empower us with the Holy Spirit to achieve what He has commissioned us to do. There is always more, but it can only come to you through the Holy Spirit.

I spent time talking about the different baptisms primarily because I was not taught that there was more in a partnership and relationship with the Holy Spirit, and you, too, might be unaware of this wonderful benefit of walking with Christ. To fully have a clear revelation of who you are in Christ, you have to know the Holy Spirit. The body of Christ has been asleep, but when the Holy Spirit touches you with His fire and power, you are forever changed and awakened to His knowledge, wisdom, and glory. The Holy Spirit is always with you, but when you allow Him to actively work through you in tangible evidence, the veil is lifted, and there is a blessing there for you and for those with whom you interact.

The Holy Spirit is incredibly important in our walk as believers because everything that we do has a purpose. We were not created in a lab as an experiment while He sits up in heaven looking down upon us, judging our every move. Likewise, we are not just to be going through the mundane motions waiting for the Lord to swoop down and rescue us from this life. He is within us and upon us to guide, protect, equip, and fulfill what we were made to do—regardless of what we believe about the different baptisms. If there is more to what I am aware that Christ is doing, I want it. If you have not been touched by the Lord in the way I have described, do not be dismayed. Ask Him for it! He is eagerly waiting for you to invite Him to encounter you in such a way.

Prayer

Holy Spirit, I invite You to come now and reveal Yourself to the person who is reading this book right now. From the top of their head to the tips of their toes, I pray for holy fire to touch them and fill them with power, love, and a sound mind. I pray that they will see miracles, signs, and wonders, and that out of their mouths will come new tongues filled with praise. I ask for more, Lord, for all of Your daughters. I ask that You would reveal the plans You have for them. Thank You for Your presence and for Your constant reminders of how You love us. In Jesus' name, amen and amen.

Your Inheritance—If You Choose

In him we also were made [God's] heritage (portion) and we obtained an inheritance; for we had been foreordained (chosen and appointed beforehand) in accordance with His purpose, Who works out everything in agreement with the counsel and design of His [own] will.

—Ephesians 1:11 amp

Reading that verse gives me the chills. Do you understand the magnitude of *who you are* as a child of God? Did you know that you are *royalty*? You are the daughter of the one true King! When Jesus died on the cross, *you* became a co-heir to the entire kingdom of heaven alongside Him. Yes, you—the one who has made mistakes in this life, the one who has been defiled and sinned against, even the one who has cursed the name of the Lord and professed that He does not exist. He paid the greatest price for you. Not one person is more important than another, but you are uniquely loved and thought of individually. You matter more to heaven than you will ever realize until you get there. You are so incredibly powerful—and if you understood a fraction of that reality, you would be able to transform a culture, a nation, and even the world.

There are many evangelists from the past that walked in supernatural gifts from the Holy Spirit that brought many into relationships with Christ, walked in miracles, signs, and wonders whom we can look to who made a cultural impact, such as Kenneth Hagin, Kathryn Kuhlman, and Smith Wigglesworth. You might be tempted to think that you are not destined or designed for that sort of work or ministry calling. But your life is a ministry—whether you work in the church or you work outside the church, you have been given a directive to spread the good news about who Jesus is to everyone you encounter in your own sphere of influence (Matt. 27). What made the great evangelists and faith leaders of the past special? I believe they told God "yes"—and then they submitted themselves and pursued an intimate relationship with Him, no matter what anyone thought. They had a greater fear of the Lord than a fear of man. I believe that God wants to pour out His Spirit upon us, anointing *all of us* with the same ability to have incredible encounters with the Holy Spirit, to dream dreams, to have visions, to prophesy, to heal the sick, to rout demons, and to perform signs and wonders in Jesus' name— not just a select few.

God doesn't need anyone to remember our names, He wants people to know and recognize Him though the actions of His everyday disciples, but we must be filled with the Holy Spirit. His works are not our works, and we can do nothing apart from Him.

In the royal families that exist on earth today, the family members must be born into their royalty. But when you are "born again" in Christ, when you accept Jesus as your Savior and acknowledge Him as Lord over your life, your DNA literally changes to become like Jesus' DNA, and you become a part of the *highest* royal lineage. This fact alone makes me realize that all of the problems I am dealing with are so small compared to who God is. The insignificance that I had placed in my mind about myself and my future changed when I realized that I am royalty and that I have a priestly duty on this earth to accomplish.

You were made to simultaneously live in heavenly places and earthly places (Eph. 2:6). You were not made for this world. This world is only temporary, and we should be seeking the Lord in how He wants to use us to fulfill the mandate of the heavenly Father in our own sphere of influence. We are all parts of the body—not one more important than another, but integral together to the fully functioning spread of the Good News to the entire land.

There is a great potential impact we can achieve as the body of Christ in this day that was unable to be achieved at any other time in history. We can use technology to reach all nations and areas of the world. What good can you do in the comfort of your own home over the internet? What if you made one small step in obedience and did something that you felt the Lord was prompting you to do, despite what others may say, and it radically changed the life of someone across the world or brought them physical, emotional, or spiritual healing?

All Power over All the Power of the Enemy

"I have given you authority to trample on snakes and scorpions and to overcome all the power of the enemy; nothing will harm you."

—*Luke 10:19 NIV*

You are a member of the royal priesthood, and that automatically comes with authority. This is not a special invitation reserved for those with the most money, the elite, or those who have a ministry.

This invitation to power and authority is given to you and anyone who leans into and desires a relationship with the Father. We should not desire a relationship with the Lord merely for the gifts we receive, but so that we can know Him intimately. He does give wonderful gifts, but the greatest gift of all is His presence and His promise of eternity to be spent with Him. When you walk in intimacy with the Father, authority and power come naturally to you because you are clothed with the presence of the Father—but it isn't just handed to you. You have to take hold of your identity, realizing exactly who you are, who has given you that identity, and what He wants you to do with it. He is always with you.

One of the greatest ways that I hear the Lord speak my identity over me is when I am praising Him, declaring His Word, and ministering to Him. I love to read scriptures aloud in my alone time with the Lord and sing to Him of His glory. Another way that I have found to grow in greater intimacy with the Father is through communion. Sure, churches routinely practice communion quarterly as a corporate body, but I never truly learned the power it holds as a weapon. Yes, taking communion and remembering the Lord's body being broken for us and His blood shed to cover all sins is a weapon because it is an act of submission and a humbling of ourselves. I come to His feet and ask Him to search my heart and reveal anything unclean so that I may repent. I remember that I can do nothing without Him, that it is only through His power and might that no weapon will be formed against me. Then I remember that His body was broken and beaten to the point that He was unrecognizable as a person, and every drop of blood was poured out and shed to wash me clean and blameless. When I remember what Christ Jesus did for me at the cross, and I give thanks to Him, I am drawn closer into His presence.

Making communion a regular part of your relationship with God, instead of primarily as a religious tradition that we do at church four times a year, will open your heart, your eyes, and your ears to what the Father is trying to say to you. It is important to practice communion as the body of Christ and we all as individuals in the body of Christ are responsible for our own intimate walk with Christ. As we make that a priority individually, and when the body of Christ comes together to do it corporately, imagine the impact that it can have! What if we are seeking intimacy with the Lord every day so that when we do come together as a church, it is like a bomb going off in the spirit? The entire community would feel it throughout the week as we continued to seek the face of the Lord and carried that to our workplace.

What excites me more than anything is bringing unity and power to the body of Christ so that it can impact the community, regions, states, and nations. Communion also has the power to bring healing. As we remember the perfect body of Jesus that was broken, and partake of the elements, we are made whole.

Another way we are given power is through prayer. Intercession and spiritual warfare is very real, and it occurs through conversation with the Father, declaring His Word over a situation or circumstance, and stepping out in faith and believing that the Lord is working on your behalf for the things you are contending for. Jesus tells us in Matthew 7:7–8: "*Ask and keep on asking and it will be given to you; seek and keep on seeking and you will find; knock and keep on knocking and the door will be opened to you. For everyone who keeps on asking receives, and he who keeps on seeking finds, and to him who keeps on knocking, it will be opened*" (amp). Many of us grow weary when we feel like our prayers seem not to be answered, but the Lord instructs us to keep seeking, to keep asking, and to keep knocking. There is power in persistence.

The way you pray and seek the Lord for all things is also important. God may have already given you the answer, which might require you to do something or step out in faith. Do you hold any unconfessed sin, or are you harboring any hate or unforgiveness in your heart? These will keep your prayers from going anywhere. We must be constantly renewed and washed clean, addressing the matters of our own hearts before we approach the heavenly Father.

You have been given the authority to use the Word of God. Your primary offensive weapon, as listed in Ephesians 6:10–18, where it talks about the armor of God, is the sword of the Spirit, which is the written Word of God, the Bible. When you consume the Word of God, meditate on it, digest it, and allow it to become a part of you, it has the ability to cut through any attack of the enemy and separate what is of this world. The Word of God is our spiritual food. We cannot live by food alone in the natural; we have to also feed our spirit with the true sustenance from heaven (Matt. 4:4). The Word of God has been misused throughout history as a weapon against people, or it has been used for the condemnation of others and how they are living their lives. This is not the intention of the true warrior of God, and we must use the sword for its intended purpose. We should never use the Word of God to hurt people; we must use it to shed light on what Satan is trying to pervert. We use it to build the body of Christ and separate evil from penetrating, killing, stealing, and destroying people, keeping them from fulfilling their intended works of God. Be careful in how you use the Word of God. Do not use it to beat anyone up, but instead use it to lift up, encourage, and edify those who are in need or who are hurting, and use it as a weapon of war against the enemy.

When Adam willingly gave up his authority to Satan, Satan took the authority of man on this earth. Jesus redeemed that by coming fully as God and fully as man, to pay for our salvation and take back our authority. We are vessels of the Lord when we accept the gift of salvation and invite the Spirit of the Lord to reside within us. We are then co-heirs with Christ, which gives us authority though Jesus. We receive this only because we have a relationship with the Lord. No authority or area of power can come to us without Christ.

Jesus tells us in John 15:5, *"Apart from me you can do nothing"* (nlt). It is He who is residing inside of you, the Holy Spirit that comes upon you that gives us power. Satan is not as powerful as we make him out to be. We tend to be frightened of him and his attacks, and we give power to his works by adding attention and fear. He also must obey the Word of the Lord, and he will run every time. The power you have been given over Satan is all-encompassing, and he only holds as much power as you give him. We cannot go around looking for enemies and devils at every turn, no, we keep our eyes on the Father and we seek to know Him and understand who we are through Him. Then when a devil shows up, you are equipped and can take authority and demand it to flee in the name of Jesus. Once you realize your authority over the enemy, the aspects of this life that bring you worry and anxiety will seem to dwindle.

Walking in your authority also involves recognizing the glory of God—when it appears and when it leaves. We can all be carriers of the glory of God, but you must walk in such a way that you do not let it break off of you. What do I mean here? It is possible to offend, or grieve, the Holy Spirit (Eph. 4:30). He is a Person with emotions, a personality, and a will (John 6:38; 1 Cor. 12:11). When we are walking in a way that is not pleasing to the Lord, it grieves the Holy Spirit. We must remain submitted to Him, be in repentance, and constantly seek His will. Some might think that living in such a way is a sign of weakness, or maybe even ignorance. The world wants us to believe that there is no God, that if we want something, we should go out and get it, and if we need to take people out on our way to the top, so be it. Having determination, hard work, dreams, and goals is not sinful. Having aspirations and desires while living a life that is submitted to God the Father and Creator of all the heavens and the earth establishes a breeding ground for greatness in your life that results in benefits to all who surround you. Jesus tells us in Matthew chapter six that we would be dominated by thoughts of worry regarding provision and the Father already knows our needs. He said to seek the Father *first* above all else, in everything, and to live righteously and He would give you everything you need (Matt. 6: 31-33 nlt).

When the Lord pours blessings out onto His children and you live submitted to Him while giving Him your desires, the Lord can launch you. When He pours out, He pours out generously so that it spills over. He wants you to walk intimately with Him and go for those aspirations with all your heart, while doing good, loving others, walking in the fruit of the Spirit, and not competing with your neighbors. If you yield and submit to God, allowing Him to have His way through you, He will do incredible works through you. Your salvation does not hinge on these deeds or works, but you are not just to be a hearer; you are to also be a doer. He knows all the desires of your heart, and He wants you to give those desires over to Him.

This creates a partnership where you can co-create something that has heavenly power behind it and is built on a solid foundation. When it gets shaken—for all things will eventually be shaken—those that are built on the foundation of Christ will remain. When you walk with the Lord in this way, you are walking with mighty power, because His power is working through you. This causes demons to flee, quakes the bowels of hell, prepares a table in front of your enemies, breaks strongholds among the people with whom you interact, shows the incredible love of the Father, and has the ability to heal the sick.

The baptism of the Holy Spirit, in my opinion, is essential for you to walk in authority. I mentioned earlier that when you accept the Lord, His Spirit resides in you for your benefit, your salvation, and your wholeness. When the Holy Spirit comes upon you, He does so for the benefit of others. I am not saying this is an absolute—there are many instances when I have had a fresh fire or a touch from the Holy Spirit that was meant for my own needs and prayers—but it always produced something in me that I could give away. Whether I was partnering with the Holy Spirit in intercession on behalf of someone, laying my hands on them and praying for healing, or if I was able to respond in gentleness when my fleshly response would have been to be angry or annoyed. Living a life consecrated to the Father, the Son, and the Holy Spirit will produce mighty power and authority as a result of your intimate relationship with Him.

You Will Do Mighty Works

And he called the twelve together, and gave them power and authority over all the demons and to heal diseases. And he sent them out to proclaim the kingdom of God and to perform healing.

— *Luke 9:1–2 NIV*

"I assure you and most solemnly say to you, anyone who believes in Me [as Savior] will also do the things that I do; and he will do even greater things than these [in extent and outreach], because I am going to the Father. And I will do

whatever you ask in My name [as My representative], this I will do, so that the Father may be glorified and celebrated in the Son."

—*JOHN 14:12–13 AMP*

"These signs will accompany those who have believed: in my name they will cast out demons, they will speak with new tongues; they will pick up serpents, and if they drink any deadly poison, it will not hurt them; they will lay hands on the sick, and they will recover."

—*MARK 16:17–18 NIV*

You were made to reflect the image of Christ, and you were given the ability to do even greater works than He did on the earth. Can you even comprehend that? In my brokenness and at my lowest point, I thought there was no way out of the pit in which I found myself. I was ready to accept it as my "new normal," thinking that maybe God just wanted me to suffer. I now know that was a lie spoken to me by Satan. The moment I hit rock bottom and was ready to die, the power of God fell on me, bringing immediate revelation. God offered me an invitation to come up higher and learn who I really was.

The creation of this book will be a surprise to many people who know me. I have chosen to keep this project close to my heart because God told me to. The Lord has invited me into a secret place to create these words with Him, where the flow and the anointing is pure and not coming from a defensive place, neither is it subject to outside negative influence. Instead, God has been training me in secret for a long time, teaching me to hear His voice and test it. I believe He knew that my tender heart was not ready for the attacks from the enemy while I was creating this book.

Words have the power of life and death. I now realize I have put up a front of strength and toughness and made people believe that not much rattles me, but I am actually very tender to the words spoken over me by other people. God brought me to a very beautiful place that separated me from all the noise that would come at me during this time. Some relationships fell away, other opportunities and desires changed, and space was created for me to learn the heart of the Father, not just for myself (which He has done and continues to do in a mighty way), but for the heart of all of His daughters. He has called me to drop all worldly judgments and stigmas and clearly see the Father's heart for everyone.

The burden and weight to feel God's love for other people is a lot to handle sometimes, especially when you have to also wrestle with your own fleshly responses. Feeling the Father's heart for someone who hates you is gut-wrenching—not only for my own tender heart, but also to feel the Father's heart to be near them and His desire to break off the pain and suffering they are experiencing.

I have sinned and treated people terribly as well; I have gossiped and not been a good friend; and when I feel the burden of the Father's heart, reminding me of what was done for me, it wrecks me. You see, not one of us deserves the Father's gift of salvation and relationship. Freely we receive, and freely we are to give. So daily, I take communion to remember the great price that was paid for my sins, and I ask that the Father search my heart and reveal anything hidden that would hinder the works of God through me, or would cause grief or offense to the Holy Spirit. I then repent and give thanks. Oh, how often I fail to meet the mark, and how often I am reminded that I can do absolutely nothing except with the grace, mercy, and power of Christ. Even just moments after repenting and rededicating my life to the Lord, I have experienced a fallen moment. Now is the time to come out of the cave and birth the works that God has been doing through me. I feel that so strongly for many daughters right now as well. The world needs your voice that was fire branded in the secret place and the wilderness and it is time to emerge into the area you are being called to.

So, do not read these words and think that you have to be perfect. The Bible is full of imperfect people whom God loves beyond comprehension, and His patience and mercy are infinite. He also loves to use unlikely and uncommon people for extraordinary conquests. If you have not experienced the secret place with the Lord, I suggest you do that. The Hebrew translation for the "secret place" is "to hide or be concealed" (*Strong's Exhaustive Concordance, 2020*). This can be a physical location – getting alone with God in a quiet place, but it is primarily a place of peace that your soul and your spirit reside in the presence of the Lord. The value of going in the secret place is explained in Psalms 91:1: "*He that dwells in the secret place of the most High shall abide under the shadow of the Almighty*" (nkjv). Going into the secret place with the Lord will allow you to remove the veil of how you *think* you should behave in front of God, and just come as you are. This creates a place for the seed He has placed in you to grow, and as the harvest comes near, He will do mighty works through you—not only for your own personal healing, restoration, and benefit, but also for those same benefits for others.

What would our days look like if when we walked into our workplace, people were being delivered from unclean spirits and being healed of all diseases? Or if everyone whom we walked past would recognize something different in us and be curious about what that was? What if everything you did pointed people to Jesus, spread love, and brought deliverance, healing, and salvation? What would it take to walk with that kind of anointing? As I have said over and over again, it takes intimacy with the Lord. We must sacrifice what we want and what we desire to live freely to Him. It looks radical, and many will not understand, but just one encounter with Jesus will flip you upside down and inside out and remove the fear of man from your life. All that you thought you knew about Jesus will be shattered, along with any religious box that you have placed Him in.

Our minds can't comprehend who He fully is or what He is capable of doing. We spend so much time trying to dissect and understand the workings and will of God, but we only come to understand more when we are in a close, intimate relationship with Him, when we are fully submitted, emptied, and dead to ourselves and full of Him. And still even then, we will not be able to fully comprehend. He just wants our yes.

When He comes asking, what will your answer be?

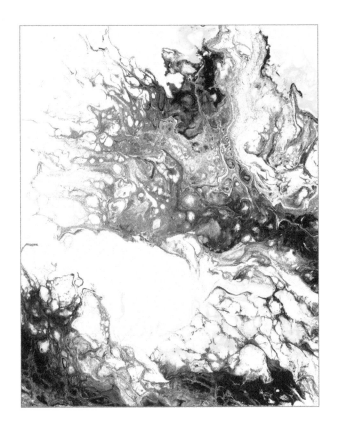

THE POWER OF
THE DECREE

Decree Defined

The definition of *decree* reads as follows: "In general, an order, edict or law made by a superior as a rule to govern inferiors. In theology, predetermined purpose of God; the purpose or determination of an immutable Being, whose plan of operations is, like himself, unchangeable" (*Webster's 1828 Dictionary*). *Easton's Bible Dictionary* provides this definition: "The decrees of God are his eternal, unchangeable, holy, wise, and sovereign purpose, comprehending at once all things that ever were or will be in their causes, conditions, successions, and relations, and determining their certain futurition. The decree being the act of an infinite, absolute, eternal, unchangeable, and sovereign Person, comprehending a plan including all his works of all kinds, great and small, from the beginning of creation to an unending eternity; ends as well as means, causes as well as effects, conditions and instrumentalities as well as the events which depend upon them, must be incomprehensible by the finite intellect of man" (*Matthew George Easton 1823–94*).

The written Word of God holds legal power in the spiritual realms. Some of the most powerful encounters and answered prayers I have ever had have come from praying and decreeing the Word of God over my life and over my family or a situation. Many people cast aside the Lord's Prayer (Matt. 6:9–13) without realizing the power and weight that it carries. By praying in the way Jesus instructed us to pray, we enter the courts of heaven with humility, honor, repentance, provision, and forgiveness. This prayer elevates us through the courts of heaven, and it ends in the war room, where we can boldly ask for the desires of our hearts, bless those who curse us, and win the spiritual war in which we find ourselves. When you repent of your sin, you successfully win your case against Satan in the courts of heaven, and you can then win the spiritual battle by decreeing the Word of God. To be maximally effective with these decrees, however, you must live a life of repentance and come to the Father, our ultimate judge.

If you ever find yourself unsure what to pray or what to say to the Father, if you are worrying about how you need to be postured to talk to Him, or if you want to see the Holy Spirit move mightily in an instant, start by praying the Lord's Prayer. I will break down this prayer and discuss how you can utilize it to posture yourself toward the Father and integrate it into a prayer that is personal to you.

Let's start in Matthew 6:9: "'*Our Father who is in heaven, hallowed be Your name*'" (nasb). We start our prayer by entering the gates of the Lord with thanksgiving and praise. When you start your prayers with thanksgiving, you are aligning your mind and heart to the Father's heart and His ways. Approach the Father on the throne in heaven and as you do, add your own adorations and words of praise toward God.

Verse 10 continues: "*Your kingdom come. Your will be done, on earth as it is in heaven*" (nasb). We have the ability to pull heaven down to earth to fulfill the mandate that each one of us has been given. What is written about you in heaven is accessible and it is imperative that we seek and ask for revelation so that His will is done through us as it is in heaven. You are declaring that in all things it is His will that matters, not ours. He cares about what is on our hearts, but we must submit to His ways, humble ourselves, and declare that it is His ways, His will, and His kingdom and we can do nothing apart from Him. To know what the desires of heaven are for this earth in your sphere of influence, you must go to the courts of heaven. As we humble ourselves to the will of the Father, we understand that He is our Provider, the One who gives us provisions in all things. This will increase your faith to know that God provides everything you need, as it goes on to state in verse 11: "*Give us this day our daily bread*" (nasb). We are told in Matthew 4:4 that "*man shall not live on bread alone, but on every word that proceeds out of the mouth of God*" (nasb). He is our Provider in all things. We are to rely on Him to provide for our common, everyday needs and provisions, as well as all of our spiritual needs. Tell Him what is on your heart and what your needs are. He already knows, but as we enter into a relationship with Him, we open up our communication and our ability to hear and receive in a fresh way. He will give you all that you need to fulfill your heavenly mandate. We can come to Him and share our requests, our needs, our dreams, and our desires. He loves to hear our hearts, and He wants to give you good gifts because He is a good, good Father. We can boldly enter the throne room, and He will not turn us away or leave us with unmet needs.

Verse 12 goes on to say, "*And forgive us our debts, as we also have forgiven our debtors*" (nasb). We must live in repentance and seek the Lord to forgive us. When we enter the courts of heaven and repent, it cancels the legal right or hold that Satan has had to use against us. Satan is our accuser (Rev. 12:10), and he stands in the courts of heaven accusing us of our sins. When we repent of our sins, both known and unknown, and we allow God to search our hearts, it demolishes the legal right that Satan has had over us. Spend some time in reflection and allow the Lord to search your heart and repent for every sin that He brings to your spirit.

The Lord's mercies are new every day, He died for all of our sins, and He became the sacrificial Lamb. We were freely forgiven for our sins, we should freely forgive others who have sinned against us. I know this may be a hard pill to swallow at times, because we tend to want to see justice served for those who do us wrong. Forgiving others is a powerful spiritual weapon. Satan will always be blown away and surprised at this because it goes against his nature. Forgiveness is the way of the Lord, and when we stand and forgive others, it annihilates the enemy's plans and brings us back into alignment with God along with repentance.

Finally, as we continue with this powerful prayer, we reach the conclusion in verse 13: "'*And do not lead us into temptation, but deliver us from evil. [For Yours is the kingdom and the power and the glory forever. Amen.]*'" (nasb). We receive protection by the blood of Jesus. He will not forsake us. His blood covers all things; it hides us from the enemy and shields us from his evil tactics to steal, kill, destroy, tempt, confuse, and pervert. After our request for protection from the enemy, we end our prayer with a bold declaration in the war room of heaven; we profess the Lord's kingdom will reign forever and ever. This statement is like the judge's gavel coming down. Everything is under the power and decree of heaven, and we move the Lord and set the angel armies in motion with our powerful decrees.

There is a difference between uttering a crafted prayer out of repetition or out of tradition and making a sincere cry from the heart. I didn't fully understand that until I was in a dark and desperate place, crying out to the Lord with everything that I had. When I was walking through the hardest moments of my life and I did not know what words to form in my prayers, the Lord's Prayer came rushing out of my mouth, and it resulted in a powerful and supernatural encounter with the Lord. Hebrews 4:16 tells us: "*So let us come boldly to the throne of our gracious God. There we will receive his mercy, and we will find grace to help us when we need it most"* (nlt).

"Pray, then, in this way:

'Our Father who is in heaven,

'Hallowed be Your name.

'Your kingdom come.

'Your will be done,

'On earth as it is in heaven.

'Give us this day our daily bread.

'And forgive us our debts, as we also have forgiven our debtors.

'And do not lead us into temptation, but deliver us from evil. [For Yours is the kingdom and the power and the glory forever. Amen.]'"

—*MATTHEW 6:9–13 NASB*

Decree and Declare

Decreeing God's Word will mobilize something into existence into your life, in your family, or on behalf of someone else or a situation. Angels are all around you, are ready to obey the Word of the Lord; they are just waiting for the order to be decreed. We have the authority to speak things into existence, but we must be rooted in the Word, know where the power is coming from and how to be in the right position to use the decree. It will not just fall into your lap because we spoke to the "universe." No, God is the Almighty, none is greater than He, and we only have power and authority because He gives it to us. Using the sword of the Spirit by speaking the Bible over our lives will change the atmosphere. It will mobilize angel armies to go to work on our behalf to accomplish the outcome that was decreed, and it will sever the plans of the enemy.

All of God's promises are yes and amen (2 Cor. 1:20). You can claim God's promises over yourself, decree them, and be confident that the Lord is working on your behalf. The Lord is not a genie in a lamp, ready to grant us wishes, and He is not at our beck and call for whenever we want something from Him. We must humble ourselves and align our prayers with His Word, His will, and His ways. That often requires a radical change in our behavior, thoughts, and posture. This will shed parts of our lives that are not of Him, thoughts we have held on to, sins that are unconfessed and not repented of, and any other areas in which we have not forgiven others—all must be addressed.

This is a time to open our hearts and allow the Lord to examine and reveal any ways we need to leave behind in order to move forward. This is a wonderful and merciful gift that the Lord gives us, because we cannot progress spiritually unless we make a change. He knows the incredible benefits that are waiting for us on the other side of leaving all of our old ways behind. He knows the plans that He has already set in motion for us, and He is just waiting for us to pick them up and turn from our old ways. Our selfish desires must die as we seek His face.

When you decree something, you are also declaring that when you pray. When you decree, you speak the law, and there is a direct action that will occur even if you don't see it. When you declare something, you prophesy or "forth tell" something into existence. The meaning of a biblical declaration is defined in the *International Standard Bible Encyclopedia* as "to make known, set forth, to give a full account, narrative, or to show" (*James Orr, 1939*). Your decreeing and declaring will allow the Word of God to be claimed as law in your life, allow the angels to fight on your behalf because they are sent to obey the Word of God, and forth-tell or prophesy that which the Lord has for you.

As a royal member of the kingdom of heaven, you have the power to decree a thing and see it be established as law (Job 22:28). The power of your words has a massive impact on whether you will physically see it or not. Whom you choose to give honor to and praise to matters. What you declare, you will manifest in your life. If you are prone to complaining or only speaking negatively about people or situations, you will manifest that in your life. Proverbs 18:20 tells us:

"A man's belly shall be satisfied with the fruit of his mouth; and with the increase of his lips shall he be filled" (kjv).

Essentially, we reap what we sow. Our words are so powerful that they can move mountains, calm storms, and heal the sick. Our words are weapons, and if used wisely and appropriately, they can do mighty damage to the bowels of hell. However, if we are speaking negative words, cursing what is good, gossiping, slandering, and complaining, we will only reap rotten fruit. Think of it like a boomerang. What we decree and declare shall come back to us. The power of life or death resides in our words—what we choose to speak in moments of conflict, anxiety, hostility, or road rage all matters. These are areas of my greatest conviction from the Lord, and I am so thankful that I have been forgiven, redeemed, and constantly renewed and reminded of this.

Remember the phrase that you were told as a kid, "Sticks and stones might break my bones, but words will never hurt me"? That is one of the greatest lies a child could ever be taught. Most of the issues that we face as adults are caused by hurts from our past and childhood pain that has not been dealt with. The power of words, when used to hurt, can deeply wound the soul. When we teach a child that we should not hold words as a concern or to simply brush off the pain they may feel from others' words, we are just suppressing something that will inevitably need to be dealt with at a later time. Teaching children to process their emotions and word wounds, and then to take them to Jesus and ask for appropriate ways to respond, would result in emotionally and spiritually intelligent adults. Imagine what we could produce or how our relationships would thrive if we had been raised in this way. We tend to build belief systems and defenses around word wounds without conscious effort. The words we speak and that are spoken to us absolutely matters; they have the ability to change the course of a person's life for the positive or negative.

These biblical principles of positive versus negative thinking and the power it holds have been perverted over time. They have become twisted and diverted to make individuals believe they have the power for their own will to be done. We do have free will, and ultimately we make our own choices, but when we speak about "decreeing something into existence," we must understand who actually holds this power. The key is to be in true alignment with the heavenly Father. We must adequately discern Satan's tactics, take authority, dethrone, and renounce them in the name of Jesus. As co-creators with Christ, we have been given authority, but we should always seek the will of the Father. Our ways are not His ways, and our mind, will, and emotions can cloud our judgment and intentions. I will be discussing this in more detail regarding the power of our thoughts in an upcoming chapter.

Activation

Here are some decrees and declarations that you can use for practice. Look up each of the verses for yourself as I reference them; it is helpful to read multiple versions of the Bible for each passage. Then apply them to your situation. What does it mean to you that God wrote these verses for *you*? Speak these out loud as you are comfortable. All of heaven, and all the angels, love to hear the Word of the Lord spoken, but evil spirits are deaf and dumb; they cannot read your thoughts, and you need to speak audibly in order for them to know who's given you authority. All of creation must bow and obey the Word of the Lord.

Don't get hung up on all of this if you do not quite understand it yet; the Lord will help you grow in this area! I was not very comfortable when I started my journey. It took time to learn more about how to pray and what happens when I do, but the Lord is so merciful, kind, and even downright giddy for you to take a leap of faith. What He will do with your silent prayers is far greater than you can imagine. Just remember, the Father knows what you are going to pray even before you do. He is not surprised about anything. Come to Him with an open heart, knowing that He is the name above every other name. Come to Him with a heart that seeks to pull heaven down onto earth. Thank Him for being your ultimate Provider; you lack nothing. Ask forgiveness and repent for any known or unknown sin and bless those who curse you. His is the kingdom and the glory and the honor forever and ever. Now we are ready to decree and declare—are you ready?

- I decree and declare that God's mighty hand is upholding me (Isa. 41:10).

- I decree that no demonic weapon formed against me will prosper (Isa. 54:10).

- I decree that I am led by the Spirit (Rom. 8:1).

- Father, I invite Your presence into my life and my home, and I declare them to be abiding places of Your glory (John 1:14).

- I decree and declare that I speak the Word of the Lord with all boldness (Acts 4:29).

- I declare that I freely forgive others and hold no offenses, so that the Lord will forgive me of my sins (Matt. 6:14).

- I decree that the Lord is able to do all things, that nothing is impossible for Him (Matt. 9:28).

- I declare that the Lord favors me, that I am His beloved, and that He made me unique and valuable (Matt. 10:30–31).

- I decree and declare that I am not troubled, that I am not afraid, and that the Lord gives me peace (John 14:27).

- I decree and declare that I am healed in the name of Jesus; God shows me mercy when I am weak and heals me when I am sick (Psa. 6:2).

- The Lord is my strength and shield. I trust Him will all my heart. (Psa. 28:27).

- Jesus died for my griefs, and He carried my sorrows. He was wounded for my transgressions, bruised for my iniquities, chastised for my peace, and by His wounds on the cross, I declare that I am healed (Isa. 53:4–5).

- I decree that I prosper in all things. My mind is healed, my body is healed, and my soul is healed (3 John 2).

- I decree that I walk with a spirit of power, a spirit of love, and a spirit of a sound mind in Jesus' name (2 Tim. 1:7).

- I declare and decree that I have the mind of Christ, and I am free from all mental oppression, shame, depression, and panic, in the name of Jesus (1 Cor. 2:16).

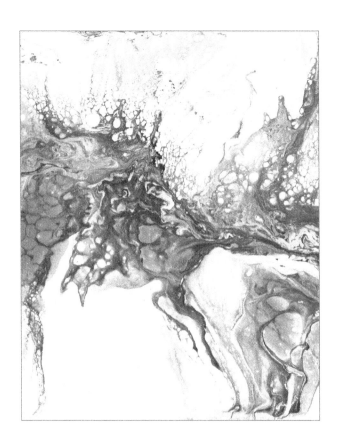

THE GOODNESS
OF GOD

Then Moses said, "I pray You, show me Your glory!" And He said, "I Myself will make all My goodness pass before you, and will proclaim the name of the Lord before you; and I will be gracious to whom I will be gracious, and will show compassion on whom I will show compassion."

—*Exodus 33:18–19* ESV

The greatest foundation in my faith is knowing that without a doubt, no matter if I am dealing with good or bad circumstances, *no matter what*, God is good. When God is referred to as "good" in the Bible it has multiple meanings in the Hebrew language that adequately encompasses the fullness in physical and spiritual meanings. It can be translated to "better, best, merry, fair, precious, fine, prosperity, beautiful, wealth, agreeable, bountiful, cheerful, at ease, ready and sweet" (*Strong's Exhaustive Concordance* 2020*)*. He does not just give these things to us, He IS all of these things. We live in a fallen, dying world riddled with sin, hatefulness, and evil, and as believers, our job is to be the bearers of His light and bring heaven to earth. We are to transform cultures despite the fallen and broken people around us. We are to bring healing, hope, and a different way of life to everyone whom we encounter. We are to show other people the embodiment of the goodness of God. This is only possible if you know who God is, who you are in Christ, the power and authority you hold, and living from a kingdom perspective—that is, seeing things from a Godlike perspective. We can only do this through a close, intimate walk with Him, seeking Him first in all things.

God does not bring evil upon this world, we live in Satan's kingdom, but we hold the power and authority through the blood of Jesus. Evil and unfathomable things absolutely do happen, and I have gone through a fair share of tragedy, pain, and trauma. I also am frequently bombarded with sorrow and compassion when I hear stories about what many people have gone through or are currently walking through, and my heart breaks for what has broken them.

I was never one to cry easily when I was growing up. My mom has told me stories from my childhood about how I would commonly bite my lower lip to prevent myself from crying, that the pain of biting my lip would override the emotional pain I was feeling. This was not beneficial for me, because I learned from a very young age to build fortresses around my heart, my mind, and my emotions. It was hard for me to allow someone past my defenses, and this has been the most difficult thing about this whole book-writing process. Feeling the hurt, grieving, or going through a process is not a bad thing, but it certainly is not easy. Deconstructing patterns from childhood is scary, but the soft heart I now hold for others and the reverence I hold for the Lord wrecks me daily. The main conclusion that I came to through this writing journey is that above all, God is good and He wants to use that pain, those hurt feelings, that brokenness to help someone else. Yes, He wants to heal you because He loves you. He wants to heal you in those areas where Satan wants to keep you stuck. He wants to shine His light on those areas to bring you blessings; you can then turn around and bring His healing to other people who are experiencing the same problems.

It doesn't matter what you have done, what anyone's opinion is of you, or what anyone else has done to you. There is a God who wants to make it right and remove the burdens and pain you are carrying. Each and every person has a horrific story of heartache they have been through—whether it be loss, death, sickness, or abuse. Your feelings, struggles, and pain are all valid. We all have the right to feel broken about our situations, but I would like to propose that we are called to live higher than these feelings of brokenness.

This concept has been difficult for me to grasp and to fully understand while I was in the midst of walking through grief. For a long time, I wanted to keep a very tight grip on my pain. I even came to the conclusion that this was just who I was. I thought that I needed to accept the shame, depression, feelings of panic, and outbursts of anger as my "new normal," my new way of life. I came to the false conclusion that everyone just needed to get used to who I was now. That was a very detrimental mind-set, and I caused a lot of damage to everyone around me because of it.

Don't do what I did. God wants to be near you, especially during these times of despair, because He promises that He will use it all for your good. Even if what caused you emotional, physical, or sexual trauma was not His original doing, He will turn all things to work for the good (or beauty, prosperity, best, fairness) of those that love Him. What a promise! We are not promised an easy life; in fact, the lives of the biblical saints are filled with persecution, imprisonment, abuse, judgment, and ridicule. That is not a life that we typically would look forward to, when you are looking at it from a worldly perspective. The lives of the believers in the Bible were not the "American dream." But they had (and we have) the opportunity to see things from a different perspective. Everything we do or do not do here on this earth has an eternal outcome, and when God shows you what that looks like, there is no earthly thing that could seem better than what He wants for you, and no one can take that away from you.

As I ponder the differences in our "Christian" culture here in the West versus the persecution that Christians in other areas of the world face on a daily basis, I realize that we are so unaware of the real danger we are in. We have every comfort imaginable, every kind of technology at our fingertips, and the freedom in this land to serve God however we choose. We have been given great favor, but that comes with great responsibility. Much is required of those who have been entrusted with much (Luke 12:48). We are not to just go through the motions and bombarded with busyness that inhibits our walk with the Lord. It is our responsibility to go after healing with all that we have, so that we can then turn to those around us and help them along the way with healing, as well. As much as we have been given, we should seek to give to others.

Spiritual Warfare

When I started to process the details of the event with my daughter and all that took place—my encounter with Jesus, hearing voices, her miraculous recovery—I was immediately attacked spiritually. Many aspects about that period of time were confusing and overwhelming, but as I continued to press in, God slowly revealed His nature and the truth to me. The spiritual attacks were predominately focused through hateful words toward myself in my mind, feelings of severe shame, depression, thoughts of suicide, PTSD, and I felt unsettled, unsure, even unhinged. I was also physically attacked with severe pain in my joints and a multitude of other debilitating health issues, such as a diagnosis of rheumatoid arthritis and a parasitic infection that brought extreme fatigue and debilitating mind fog. I was having issues with caring for the kids as my husband worked long hours. I had lost my strength to grip in my hands, and I was numb from my fingers to my elbows.

As if that was not enough, I was also being spiritually demonized in my home. We were having several encounters with demons in the house terrorizing us, and I was not the only one experiencing those events. Satan was pulling out all the stops to get me to turn against God and inevitably end my life, because he knew that once everything came into alignment and I realized the truth—about who I was, what God did for me and my daughter, and the plans that God intended for me through this situation—he would be demolished. I was a warrior, and I did not even know it. The enemy was already defeated when Jesus died on the cross; this situation that I was battling had already been nailed to the cross and then buried with Jesus. Deuteronomy 31:8 gives us a promise that is still relevant today. I paraphrase and pray it over you as this: *Sister in Christ, God already has gone before you, and He will be with you while you are walking through trials of all kinds, He will never leave you, and He will not forsake you (or abandon you, flee from you, cast you away). He gives very clear directions to you not to be afraid or discouraged. In every circumstance, He went before me in my struggles, and He knew that this would be a turning point in my life. He opened my eyes at the perfect time to see that, and I know that He will do the same for you. Amen.*

God taught me how to go to war in the Spirit, and He brought people into my life to guide me along the way. I never knew my mom was a powerful intercessor and warrior in the kingdom. I came to learn just how intricately God made my mom and I to be sensitive to His nature and will and that we were far more powerful together than we were independent of each other. God opened my eyes and my heart at the perfect time so that I could grow deeper in the relationships in my life, but ultimately also grow my intimacy and trust with Him. It all started with learning who I was and the authority I had. Matthew 18:18 says: *"Truly I tell you, whatever you bind on earth will be bound in heaven, and whatever you loose on earth will be loosed in heaven"* (esv). When you bind and loose on this earth, that is an authoritative decree. Wimpy prayers are not allowed; they will continue to go unanswered because they hold no power, authority, or directive. They do not move heaven, and they do nothing to quake hell. Repeating prayers like, "Jesus, if it is Your will, please heal my mind," will have no effect. No, healing was already secured for you, and you do not have to question whether it is His will. It absolutely is. He already told you, "It is finished." You are a saint, and when you declare a thing, it shall be established. You were made for mighty works. Satan and all of his demons must bow to the authority that has been given to you through the blood of Jesus. You have been given all power and authority over all the power of the enemy, and you must declare and decree the Word of the Lord, because it is the law. The written Word of God must be apart of you. Spend time and actively digest the words and allow the Lord to speak to you through it. In perilous times, it is imperative that you know how to use the sword that you were given. I believe that legions of angels are at the ready on your behalf and just waiting for the order to be spoken.

It is up to each one of us to realize our identity and grow and mature to fulfill the mandates on our lives. Once I realized who I was, figuring out what I was created for was no longer a question. The plans the Lord had been speaking to me my entire life all of a sudden made sense. Sometimes we do not know exactly what we are up against or how to pray, or we are in so much pain that nothing comes out when we try to pray. Silent prayers or prayers that cry out are not wimpy prayers if you are posturing your heart toward the Lord. Wimpy prayers are those that do not understand the nature, will, and power of God and are void of the Holy Spirit. Where the Holy Spirit is, there is power. Now, God can use our anguish and our cries to Him as a powerful weapon in the Spirit. I am simply saying that the power in a prayer comes from the Holy Spirit, and He gives you your identity based on you living a life from repentance and understanding your authority over Satan, seeking the heart of the Father in all things. Ask for a fresh revelation of His will for the situation moving forward, and if you still do not have the words to say, just submit to Him, giving it all and laying it at His feet. Every act of humbling yourself before the Lord moves Him. He is just waiting for your yes. He is so close and near you even if it does not seem like He is. He is working on your behalf regardless if you can feel or see the evidence of Him at the moment. Our timing is not His timing and thoughts of the Lord's delay are usually our misrepresented personal will mistaken for His will. His timing is always perfect and I encourage you to keep pressing in and seeking the Lord. Fasting is a wonderful way to getting answers from the Lord. Some deliverance only comes through fasting and praying. Fasting is not a diet and it is a personal decision that you make with the Lord. Length and nature of the fast should be done through communication with the Father.

As this process unfolded for me, there was an acceleration in seeing, hearing, and sensing aspects of God and things not of God all around me. I was seeing things in the spirit that you might see in a horror movie, but I was also witnessing the most beautiful visions as well. The spiritual realm is very real, and it runs parallel to the natural world in which we are living and interacting. There are angels and demons at work all around us—far more than you realize. It is both fascinating and terrifying at the same time to experience these things, and I am still learning, yielding, and pressing in more and more each day.

I am not sure that my experience will be exactly your experience upon reading this, but it was mine, and it has made my childhood make more sense, especially how I just knew things that I would not have known otherwise about people and circumstances, or how things worked or operated that I did not previously understand. Your personal journey is one that will blossom as you grow in intimacy with Jesus, as you draw closer to His nature, His character, and His will for your life. What did He create that is unique about you? What are the interests that keep pressing in on you—even if they don't hold a monetary value? As I explored these areas in my life, I realized how creative I was. I have always been a dancer, but I am also an artist. I had shelved that talent for a long time, especially after having children, because it is a time-consuming hobby. But then the Lord spoke to me and told me that I am a painter and that He would give me visions from heaven to help those who are dealing with trauma in their lives. As I painted these visions, they would touch people and bring healing to their hearts.

Human Error

Not all things that happen to us are direct attacks from Satan, as much as it feels good to blame him for everything. Sometimes we ourselves make bad decisions, or a series of bad decisions. As I was birthing this book, I was spiritually attacked, but during that time I also made a lot of mistakes while trying to navigate all of it, and these worsened the attacks, or at the very least, prolonged them. I have made devastating errors throughout my whole life, and I will continue to make bad choices—because I am human. I was born a sinner, but I am living with conviction and owning my mistakes.

Living in repentance and seeking God's will for all areas of our lives is very important for our spiritual walk and growth. When we are the most vulnerable, we are open for attacks, and when we are living life from a selfish place of a survival mentality, the thoughts and feelings of others tend to not be our primary concern. In many instances, I was incapable of thinking of anyone else. This is not an excuse for my behavior or to lighten the damaging effects I had on the people whom I love. It is actually the opposite. It is a very humbling experience to come to the place where you realize you have hurt people and to seek forgiveness not knowing whether or not it will be accepted.

If you have made a mistake, no matter how big or small, God wants to restore you in that area. I feel Him saying that right now, as you are reading this, you should confess it out loud to Him and repent of your involvement with it, and He will take it away. He loves to use our brokenness, our mistakes, as a launching pad to help others on similar journeys. Satan loves to come in and highlight those areas where we have made errors and bring ridicule and shame into our lives. I would like to suggest that those areas in which you are feeling the greatest shame, those are the areas in which God would like to launch you into your greatest ministry—and your greatest blessing. God has already defeated Satan. The battle is already won, and I cannot say that enough. God wants to show off for you—just like when our kids make mistakes and it becomes a teachable moment to help them grow. God uses our mistakes much in the same way, to help build our character as we become more of a reflection of Jesus. As we press in, it gives Him an opportunity to circumcise our hearts, create newness in us, and download wisdom so that we can then bless those around us.

He Makes All Things Good

God absolutely will turn all things for good, but He also wants to refine you and mold you into becoming more and more Christlike. Be careful what you ask for, however. If you are struggling with anger or patience, He will give you opportunities to respond in the opposite way. In situations where you have previously been angry or impatient, He will help you to build your character, cancel any plans of the enemy, and lawfully cancel the accuser of the brethren's case against you in the courts of heaven (Rev. 12:10). This opportunity is a time to pause, reflect, and make a choice to walk in the fruit of the Spirit. These nine fruit are listed in Galatians 5:22–23: "*But the fruit of the Spirit is love, joy, peace, patience, kindness, goodness, faithfulness, gentleness, self-control; against such things there is no law*" (nasb). The fruit of the Spirit will counter *every* attack of the enemy; there is no defense against it. No law can be written to override its power. Walking in the fruit of the Spirit will also cancel any tactic of the enemy to trip you up, torment you, or tempt you in that area. God will always walk in the opposite spirit from the enemy. So, when you are met with a situation in which you are prone to become angry, pause and choose instead self-control and love. If you usually respond with a sharp tongue, choose instead to slow down and exercise gentleness. I urge you to keep trying, even if you have moments when you fail. In fact, I can say with all certainty that you absolutely *will* fail, but God will always show up when you choose His fruit, and with practice, these will be your new nature and character traits.

Imagine the blessings if we, as the church, exercised these in every situation in our lives—especially the workplace. It does not matter how many times we fail, He will give us the opportunity to pass the test again and again, over and over until we get it right. He is such a loving, patient, and merciful God. Most of the time we do not recognize these refining moments of character building, and we try to rebuke them as something from Satan.

I know many people—my husband, for example—who faithfully walks in the fruit of the Spirit. It is absolutely my husband's nature and character, and when there is a moment that he responds outside of this, I know that something is wrong or weighing on him. We are not perfect—only Jesus is—but if we have made this a lifestyle and it is our character to walk in love, genuinely have joy, seek peace, practice patience with those that trigger us, respond with kindness when someone is unkind, give with goodness while knowing that we lack nothing, honor our word with faithfulness, and maintain control over our thoughts, emotions, and actions—a moment when we walk outside of that is an opportunity for us to intercede and come alongside each other with that same fruit to offer encouragement and cover each other in prayer. In my darkest moments, times when I was really unlovable, my husband freely showed me who I really was—my identity in God, whether he knew it or not—by how he responded to me. This, my friends, is how we are to engage with our neighbors, just as we are commissioned to do.

When I went through this struggle in my life, some pretty awful things about my character were highlighted that had been repressed, likely stemmed from a young age. The Lord brought me to the place where I could no longer control, hide, or escape these flawed aspects of my character. The impurities of my heart had to be revealed so that I could submit them to the Father, repent, and allow Him to purify those facets of my heart. It took me awhile to recognize that this was *not* a spiritual attack from the enemy, but an opportunity from my good, loving Father to refine me and take me where He needed me to be. I am so thankful for those who truly love me. God surrounded me with people in my life to build me up, and He removed individuals who could not support me during this time, who only meant harm during this process.

Going through this journey was not a comfortable time in my life. It hurts to let go of relationships, even if they are not productive or are detrimental. There is also pain in the realization of our flaws, but the Lord does not condemn; He corrects and gives us the opportunity over and over to choose Him. Permit the loving and faithful God to refine you, and be open to the process, which is uncomfortable and complex, of becoming more Christlike. As you seek the Lord during these times, ask Him to give you supernatural peace and joy that will carry you through. The humbleness and humility that is produced on the other side of character building is pleasing to the Lord.

As I went through this testing, character building, and refinement, I was met with a very challenging situation in which I was attacked. I was immediately very emotional, and anger filled every cell in my body. It brought me in an instant back to ground zero, but after some time of wrestling solo with it, I heard the Lord say to me, *"This is a defining moment, a turning point. How will you respond?"* So I repented for allowing myself to go back to that place from which I had been redeemed, and I prayed a blessing over the person who meant harm to me and my livelihood, giving it all to the Lord. I was rescued, and the victory was already won. I did not have to do anything except thank the Lord for guarding me, sending angels on my behalf, and giving me the opportunity to show someone the love of Jesus in return. I did not have to seek retaliation or justice. He will always use something that meant us harm for good. We have a divine inheritance against attacks, as stated in Isaiah 54:17: *"'No weapon forged against you will prevail, and you will refute every tongue that accuses you. This is the heritage of the servants of the Lord, and this is their vindication from me,' declares the Lord"* (niv). Amen. We have an Advocate who walks within us, alongside us, and if we allow Him to do so, He will guide us on the straight and narrow path toward freedom and salvation (Matt. 7:14).

I am far from perfection in this, and I fail more times than I succeed, but I am thankful for grace and mercy that allows me to continually get up again and brush myself off. I can repent from where I veered off the path, turn back toward Jesus, and make another attempt. I am a warrior, and no matter how many times I get beaten down,

I will always—with bruises, abrasions, and wounds—get back up again and seek the One who paid for it all. I will always keep going forward.

Regarding the scenario I mentioned, which produced an extremely strong emotional response in me from which I thought I had been freed, I pressed in through prayer and cried out for help, and the following is what I wrote down in my journal: a love letter of encouragement from my loving Father in heaven. I pray that it blesses you as well.

It is a turning point!

You have contended and presented your case to Me. You have repented and warred. You have loved and blessed. When light shone on your darkness and sin, you did not blame. You took ownership. Tests have come to refine you. The bringing up of pain from the past has done a few things: It caused you to remember how far you have come in spiritual growth, and it presents a door. Will you walk through it, or will you succumb to the flesh or worldly ways and seek justice in return for false accusations? This is a pivotal point, a tipping point, to exponential blessing, promotion, and joy. It is going to take everything you have. Keep pushing, keep renewing your mind to My truth. Continue to bless those who curse you. Step into your identity once and for all. Your character will be made known. I will prepare a table in front of your enemies, and judgment will be Mine, says the Lord. Keep interceding for your enemies. Do not boast. The fear of the Lord is upon you. Darling daughter, I am so proud of you. Your initial reaction was of the flesh, but through wisdom imparted to you through My Spirit, you heard Me. Keep going. I am with you. No weapon formed against you shall prosper. Put on the full armor that I have supplied for you each and every day. As you do, the fiery arrows will not touch you, not even close. Prepare for the new wind. I love you.

That is how awesome and good the Father is. He wants to communicate with you just like that. Do not grow weary if you feel like you are not hearing the Lord like this right now. It took me awhile in going through tests and seeking to figure out what was coming from my thoughts and what was from the Lord, and even still, I am in a growing season. We never fully have God figured out, and our relationship with Him is constantly growing deeper if we are committed to Him. As we grow deeper, revelatory knowledge abounds, and He releases and imparts what He chooses. In another chapter, I will give you an exercise to walk you through hearing the Lord for yourself, and how to distinguish His voice more clearly over time.

BATTLE OF THE MIND

Your Thoughts Matter

For as he thinks in his heart, so is he.

— *Proverbs 23:7 NKJV*

Do not be conformed to this world, but be transformed by the renewal of your mind, that by testing you may discern what is the will of God, what is good and acceptable and perfect.

— *Romans 12:2 ESV*

Self-help and the power of positivity has gained a lot of ground, not only in the secular world, but in church circles as well. While it sounds nice that God will fulfill our every desire, want, and wish, that is not biblical. The lives of believers throughout the Bible are not filled with stories of wealth, dream jobs, and extravagant lifestyles. What we see are people dying to their fleshly desires, taking up their cross, and following Jesus—some at the cost of their actual lives. We cannot save ourselves, no matter how much we wish for it, plan for it, or schedule it into our day. Living for the Lord involves a spiritual battle, and it requires a full relinquishment on our part to a big God.

When I Googled the phrase "positive thinking," 93.9 million hits popped up in a matter of seconds. What is interesting to me is that none of the pages that I sifted through mentioned Jesus anywhere. Some prosperity concepts were evident, but Jesus Himself was never mentioned. If any of them actually mentioned a biblical concept, the message was twisted in some way. The power of arresting your thoughts and using "positive thinking" is a biblical concept that has been diverted, perverted, and commercialized, and many believers have freely bought into a principle that is full of deception. Philippians 4:8 says, *"And now, dear brothers and sisters, one final thing. Fix your thoughts on what is true, and honorable, and right, and pure, and lovely, and admirable. Think about things that are excellent and worthy of praise"* (nlt). We must set our minds on things above, aligning our thoughts with God's thoughts, not with what is happening on this earth (Col. 3:2). God's thoughts are not in alignment with what the world says, He challenges us in our spiritual growth and corrects us to get us back on track. As I have mentioned before, God is a good God. He IS good, He IS prosperity, He IS abundance, but He is the God of order as well. Blessings and abundance come with a process and it requires humility, repentance, obedience, and submission. Can God trust you with what you are asking to carry and do you know the ramifications of carrying it? This tempering process does not usually make us feel warm and cozy inside until we acknowledge and make the effort to alter our path. Accessing the thoughts of God requires friendship with the Father, building a relationship and history with Him, and actively studying the Word of God. He wants to speak to you more than you want to hear from Him. He has been constantly speaking to us our whole lives, but we are just not tuned in to the sound of His voice. It is a lot like manually searching for a radio station; you get a lot of feedback and static, or dead airwaves (silence), if you are not tuned in to the right channel. Getting calibrated to His voice comes from a place of humility, repentance, obedience, and submission. The Lord does not just speak to us in positive thoughts or concepts that make us feel good inside. The Bible is filled with challenging concepts that do not elicit positive thoughts or feelings, but those are not to be rebuked as false doctrine. Our ways are not His ways; our thoughts are not His thoughts. My personal journey over the last several years has been a breaking down of thought processes that seemed to sound like they came from God, but they did not. We must be open to challenging our minds and filtering them through the cross.

Many Christ followers get trapped here in believing that they do not have to be submitted to God in this area. We have already established that we can do nothing apart from Christ. We know that He infinitely loves His daughters and that He has granted all power and authority over all power of the enemy to those who believe. We are absolutely powerful, and what we think and what we say is important, but all things—including our thoughts, affirmations, decrees, and proclamations—must be submitted to the One who is the ultimate judge. God absolutely loves how powerful His daughters are—He made us that way! However, it is vital to know who we are and what our ultimate mission is in Christ. We must have our feet firmly planted on those principles.

If we hold all that power, we need to know how to wield it so that it is effective and powerful against the enemy, building the kingdom of God and not partnering with the enemy to pervert God's ways. People usually use the power of positive thinking in a way to manifest more money into their lives. God is not a genie in a lamp, ready to grant our wishes of fame, wealth, and power for the sake of our wanting it. Everything we do and think matters, including what we choose to partner with and the theologies behind it.

If something is founded on a basis that is not of Jesus, then it is evil— no matter how beautifully it is wrapped or how good the message makes us feel. Second Corinthians 11:14 states: *"And no wonder, for Satan himself masquerades as an angel of light"* (niv). We are called to be constantly vigilant because Satan is the ultimate deceiver. We should be asking each day for keen discernment and to be as wise as a serpent and as harmless as a dove (Matt. 10:16). Sometimes the most profound messages are the ones that pierce through us with a double-edged sword instead of tickling our ears. Simply speaking your hopes and dreams out into the universe, believing that "something out there" will somehow compel the universe, or whatever higher power you align with, to do your bidding, to make all the stars align for you or for others to magnetically be attracted to you, is not of God and I see many professing Christians fall into this trap. This is perversion wrapped in a giant lie from the enemy to take your focus off God and make you believe that you are alone the creator of your life and your future. The creator of all things, God, does want to give you your heart's desires beyond your wildest dreams, and the power of the decree is absolutely powerful, but I get the sense that He is asking, *"Am I enough?"* Is the presence of the Lord in your life enough and valued over material things? Are you willing to go through the process that the Lord has planned for you? As previously mentioned, it will require obedience, submission to His will, and repentance. A life lived in this way automatically is a heart drawing closer to the heart of the Father, which naturally abounds in blessings flowing on you. In Matthew 7:9–11, Jesus asks: *"Which of you, if your son asks for bread, will give him a stone? Or if he asks for a fish, will give him a snake? If you, then, though you are evil, know how to give good gifts to your children, how much more will your Father in heaven give good gifts to those who ask him!"* (niv). God wants to give us more than we could imagine, but He is not here to complete our mission or to just make us prosperous. We are here to fulfill His mission, and the provisions, talents, gifts, and anointing that He gives to us are for the sake of our own healing and the healing, deliverance, and salvation of others—all for His glory. We will only receive what He wants to give to us, which does exceed our every desire, but the purpose of that is to point people back to Him and His power, not our own.

We do have absolute authority over the enemy, but we only have authority through the blood of Jesus. His Word is law, and decreeing His words over our lives does move mountains, changes atmospheres, and sets angels at the ready to fulfill what is written. I absolutely believe in decreeing and praying for health, wealth, protection, provision, and all of our dreams to bring them into existence, because that is who God is as a good Father. But we need to realize who the Author truly is, where all gifts come from, and discern what they are to be used for. Who is the ultimate One that gives and takes away (Job 1:21)? What would be the point of giving you a stream of wealth if you are not a good steward of what has already been given to you? What is the point of declaring powerless words out into thin air? We want to see the real manifestation of the glory of God, right? We must come from a place of humility and repentance, and we must be mission – and kingdom-driven for the plans that God has for us.

That might not mean having your own personal jet or whatever it is that you wrote on your dream board last year. How can you know if it is the will of God unless you are in a close relationship with Him? What does He want you do with what you already have? Get good at being an adequate steward of whatever He has already streamed into your life, and there will be more. There is always more. As you learn how to decree and discover the power that holds, if you are in alignment with the Word of God, you will see far more powerful moves of God than simply just speaking positive words over yourself and your family.

Battleground

Be alert and of sober mind. Your enemy the devil prowls around like a roaring lion looking for someone to devour. Resist him, standing firm in the faith, because you know that the family of believers throughout the world is undergoing the same kind of sufferings.

—1 Peter 5:8–9 NIV

I am going to step out on a limb and say that the greatest spiritual warfare battles that we face are not in the form of physical demonic attacks, but they are the constant demonic attacks on our minds. We are constantly being bombarded through what we see with our eyes and what we hear with our ears. These are direct gateways to our minds, where thoughts, pictures, and messages are dissected, translated, and made conscious. It is extremely important to be vigilant to what we watch and listen to. The thoughts that we think and allow to fester can take on a life of their own, it seems. Have you ever had something come across your mind and it immediately draws an emotional response? Your mind then starts cataloging the many instances when this would be true, so then it becomes real and true to you. This happens a lot when we speculate about the actions of another person, talk about hot political topics, or read the tone of a text message in a way that the sender did not intend to imply. Our minds, wills, and emotions are not fully reliable if we have not transformed, renewed, and discerned God's will in the matter.

For myself, I get attacked in my mind regarding my children and my inability or lack of skill in an area that I feel called or led into. God does correct us, but He will never condemn and ultimately He cares about the matters of the heart. The Lord will ask us to do things that we alone cannot accomplish in our own power. We must test our thoughts because Satan's primary method of attack is deception. He does this by presenting ideas or thoughts, maybe through people, with ideas that are half true, twisted, or perverted. When we take a deception from the enemy and we accept it as true, it starts the formation of a wall around our heart, as a barrier or a separation from God. After agreeing with enough lies, you have built a fortress that not only acts as a pretend barrier from the Lord (I say "pretend" because He can break any stronghold). The goal of the enemy by bombarding your gates is to ultimately access and infiltrate your heart. It is vital that we guard our hearts, apply the full and complete armor of God and ensure that deception is not coming in by what we are willfully seeing and hearing for entertainment purposes.

The biggest issue is that this separates us from seeking the Father for the ultimate Truth. There is only one capital *T* Truth, and it comes from Jesus. We must earnestly seek the Father. He has given us free will, and He wants us to seek Him. He is always present for us at the ready, chasing us down, but if we have only believed a lie and have not tested it, how would we possibly be able to discern the ultimate Truth, which is God? What we harbor in our minds flows through the heart, and it is ever more urgent in this time and season to ask God to search our hearts and reveal any lie that we have partnered with. This is a war, a battle of flesh versus spirit; it is very real and immediate, and drastic measures need to take place. The reality of this war has never been more abundant than what we are experiencing today. Lawlessness and evil are being seen as "good" and the move of God and the rising of righteous people that carry the heart of the Father are seen as "selfish."

We must learn to take each thought captive and test it against what God says. He will never contradict His written Word. If you are getting a conflicting message and it goes against what the Scriptures say, you can immediately bind that thought and ask the Lord to replace it with His Truth. This does not mean that God will not give a challenging word that might catch you off guard or challenge a way of thinking that you have clung to that is not of Him. There are plenty of passages in the Bible to get offended at, and we should seek to understand His heart behind them in full context of the Bible and seek Him for wisdom and knowledge. When we are confronted with something that we might discern in the beginning to be negative, God might be trying to deconstruct something in us that needs to go. All thoughts that go against the Word of God must be bound, arrested, and rebuked. Rejoicing in the Lord and all He has done is a wonderful way to begin to bring your thoughts into divine alignment.

Mourning and feeling the heart of God for others is not the same as having negative thoughts. The Lord absolutely grieves and has emotions. Many "positive" thoughts are against the will of God, as well. We should seek to have discernment in all things, especially over the matters of the mind. I am not saying that we should ever be false about what we are feeling. I am saying that our minds are deceitful, and Satan uses them as a breeding ground to infiltrate our lives and our actions. Renewing our minds to what the Lord says about the world, His nature, and our identity is vital in having clarity. As members of the army of God, we will be far more powerful if we can immediately sense an attack from the enemy before it has time to take root. That only comes from practicing hearing from God, discerning what is of Him and what are our thoughts, areas where Satan has used our eyes, ears, and mind to deceive us, and challenging ourselves by meditating on the living Word of God. It is especially important to meditate on the passages that confuse or challenge our thought processes.

Another tactic of Satan is to bring about condemnation. Condemnation attempts to make you feel like you have done something wrong, that you have missed God, that you have been cut off from His favor, that He does not care about you or your future, that He does not exist in your day-to-day life, and that you have messed up beyond repair or reprieve. This might come in the form of words from people or thoughts in your own mind. This is rampant across all social media, and you may feel gaslighted—which means to be manipulated into questioning your own sanity if you do not hold "mainstream," or worldly, ideas. This attack is rampant over ideals of the church and believers all over the world. Condemnation breeds hopelessness and is never from God. Conviction is a different concept; it is from the Holy Spirit. The word *conviction* does mean that you are found guilty just as if you were convicted of a crime, but the deeper biblical meaning is that it becomes a revelatory knowledge of your sin so that you can repent and turn from those ways (*Strong's Exhaustive Concordance* 2020). God highlights these areas not to show us and make us feel guilty, but He reveals them so that we can turn away and move closer to Him, come up higher and learn His ways, and eventually become more and more like Him. We can bring sin to the cross because Jesus already paid for it, and He brings forgiveness; ultimately this creates an area in which we can bless others. "*He is faithful and just to forgive you your sins and to cleanse you from all unrighteousness*" (1 John 1:9 niv).

Responding with the fruit of the Spirit is a greater weapon to the enemy and a breeding ground to the thoughts of God than any spiritual gift is. Just as I mentioned in the previous chapter, these are things we choose: love, joy, peace, patience, kindness, goodness, faithfulness, gentleness, and self-control. Nothing on this earth can come against or challenge the fruit of the Spirit. We are being challenged to think in every circumstance, and the matters of our hearts and thoughts as responses should reflect the Lord that resides on the inside of us. The beliefs that we hold about who God is and our identity in Him will drive all aspects of life, good or bad.

Think Again

And do not be conformed to this world, but be transformed by the renewing of your mind, so that you may prove what the will of God is, that which is good and acceptable and perfect.

—*Romans 12:2 NASB*

Have you ever wondered what it means to "not be conformed to this world"? Turn on the television to any news channel or open up social media, and it will not take you long to learn what the overall message is of this world is in it most simplistic forms: fear, sin, hopelessness, hostility, and division. On a deeper level, you can feel the draw to question the nature or reality of God, and you may have heard people ask that if there is a God, how would He allow such vile things to happen. Maybe you have questioned that very thing after being under immense pain and attack in your own life or after witnessing horrible things happen to those you love. Children dying of cancer has been an area where I needed to seek God in counsel about this as well. I don't have all the answers here, but here is what I do know: God is the Creator; Satan perverts creation. God is good; Satan is evil. God is love; Satan is hate. God is life; Satan is death. God is truth; Satan is a liar. God does not cause evil to happen in this world, but we have been given free will, and the choice is all of ours in how we will use what God has given us. Some choose to use this free will to do bad things or they use it for the works of the Lord. Our choices matter in every aspect of life, and there is always a counter-consequence. Being good stewards of this land, our bodies, our minds, our souls, and our spirits is up to each individual. As we are renewed individuals, we come together as a collective body, the church, to make a global impact. Even making impacts in your community or in your home matters a great deal. God will utilize those broken places in our lives, be encouraged with that. Whether you are fractured or you are crumbled to dust, the Lord will use those broken places to propel you forward just as He did with Jacob when he wrestled with the Lord. He would not let go until he got his blessing. He had a physical injury that resulted from this wrestle and Israel was birthed out of it (Gen 32:22 – 32).

Search me, O God, and know my heart! Try me and know my thoughts! And see if there is any grievous way in me, and lead me in the way of the everlasting.

— *PSALM 139:23–24 ESV*

We must learn to challenge what goes on in our mind and "think again." What I mean is, if you have a thought that is not of God, take hold of it and immediately replace it with another thought. We are instructed to take every thought captive in 2 Corinthians 10:4–5: "*For the weapons of our warfare are not of the flesh, but divinely powerful for the destruction of fortresses. We are destroying speculations and every lofty thing raised up against the knowledge of God, and we are taking every thought captive to the obedience of Christ*" (nasb). All knowledge and wisdom come from God, and He gives as He deems fit. Every thought should be tested against what God says.

Activation

I encourage you to spend some time and write out every negative thought or feeling that comes to you; do this for one day. Find a counter-verse by cross-referencing that emotion in the Bible. You could simply put in an internet search engine: "*What does the Bible say about* _____—whatever it is that you are feeling. It will generate several verses that will reference the concept or emotions that you are feeling. Write those verses out and meditate on them. Say them aloud over and over again, and "chew" on them and digest them. Allow the Lord to reveal something to you, and spend time journaling what He reveals to you and hold fast to that. The Word is alive and active, and a verse that you might gloss over because you have it memorized, still holds new revelations from the Lord. Doing this activation has opened my eyes, my heart, and ears to receive more revelation. The Lord loves to speak to us through the

BATTLE OF THE MIND

Scriptures, and I pray that you are blessed by doing this and making it a part of your life.

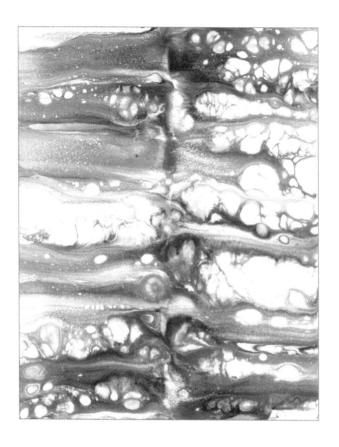

JOY IN THE BATTLE

Is It Possible to Have Joy in the Midst of a Battle?

It tells us in James 1:2 to *"consider it pure joy, my brothers and sisters, whenever you face trials of many kinds"* (nasb). If you have lived on this planet for a moment, then you know that trials, tests, health scares, tragedy, and loss do not feel joyful. It is a stretch for many of us who have ever gone through trials to consider it pure joy. In fact, I feel like I have done a pretty good job of practicing the opposite my entire life. I have pondered this verse countless times through this particular season in my life because I was already wrestling with shame of not being happy that we had a good outcome with almost losing our daughter, but I could not seem to pull myself out of a state of gloom. *Where was my joy, and why was I unable to just create it out of thin air? Even deeper still, Lord, why must I find it "pure joy"?* What I realized was that I simply was not in tune with the promise that the passage goes on to state. It goes on to tell us in verses 2 and 3: *"Because you know that the testing of your faith produces perseverance. Let perseverance finish its work so that you may be mature and complete, not lacking anything"* (nasb). A tragedy is not joyful, hardships are not joyful, losses are not joyful, but there is a promotion on the other side of it all, and we are on a journey of growth and maturing through the circumstances that we face. The perseverance of the testing of our faith makes us mature and complete, inevitably making us more and more like Jesus.

If we can endure for a season, keep our eyes on Jesus, and persevere, there is the promise of a next level. Not only will we get through it, but Jesus will elevate us, He will give us kingdom wisdom and insight (maturity), and He will make us complete by using those broken places for good. We will lack nothing.

Once I walked through my trial, the first thing I felt was completely and fully loved. Wisdom and insight from the Lord were revealed over time, and it continues to be revealed as I walk through this journey of life with Him. What I have experienced over this season of my life is that when I sense pressure building in my spirit, when I start to feel the pang of panic arising, or when I keep getting kicked down, I can stop and thank Jesus for what He is about to do. He doesn't bring us calamity, but He promises us that He will work *all* things for our good (Rom. 8:28).

Isn't that exciting? God is for you, and if He is for you, who could possibly be against you? (Rom. 8:31). I know that might be hard to hear if you are currently walking through a difficult season, but all of God's promises are yes and amen. He will never forsake you. It tells us in Psalm 30:5 that *"weeping may stay for the night, but rejoicing will come in the morning"* (niv). There are seasons when we will feel broken, we will feel sad, and we will miss the mark. God does not tell us to be fake and pretend to be happy and joyful all the time, He knows we live in a sad and fallen world. His own heart breaks for the lost, the sick, the widows, the orphans, and all of what worries you. He died and bore the pain of all your pain, your circumstances, and the evil of the world. His resurrection gives us resurrection—a new life, a new way, and eternity with Him. We can hold tightly on to every promise that He has given to us. He will not leave you, and He will get you through this season. He wants to teach you so much through this journey that you never would have been able to absorb at any other time in your life. You are going to get paid back seven times what was stolen. You are going to learn something new and at a deeper level, and you will gain wisdom and insight directly from the Father's heart if you just keep moving and keep your eyes on Him. Hold on to those promises, and when you get on the other side and you understand the magnitude of Him holding on to His promises, when you face another problem, you can then consider it with joy in your heart that He has something absolutely amazing for you on the other side. When you find the weight crushing you, lay it at the Father's feet and continue to seek Him. Keep knocking and asking. It will not be easy, and it might be painful along the way, but He is going to make it all worthwhile in the end.

I love the analogy of a grape getting crushed to make wine or an olive into olive oil. In order to produce the end product that many utilize and enjoy, the fruit had to be crushed on all sides. It is vital that we recognize these moments in our lives so that we do not grow weary. Even though our natural bodies age each day and will eventually die, the spirit inside of each of us has the ability to be renewed each and every day. The trials and afflictions that we face day in and day out produce the oil we need to bless others, as well as give us an eternal glory that the Bible says *"is far beyond comparison"* (2 Cor. 4:16–17 niv). We can also look to our present circumstances as pure joy because they are temporary, and what is produced from the trials we face is eternal (2 Cor. 4:18). We have been given all that we need to be conquerors, and God will never leave us or hang us out to dry. It might seem like He is quiet at times, and that can be uncomfortable. In those times, I try and go back and determine what was the last thing the Lord spoke to me. Sometimes we are seeking new answers when He has already given us the blueprints and all the ingredients we need to make what He instructed to happen. We cannot be complacent and sit idly by, expecting the Lord to move on our behalf. We must be doers, and when we step out in faith, it gives Him room to meet us there and give us more.

Are You Due?

I learned through these last few trials that one of my greatest sources of joy during times when I feel attacked by the enemy, is knowing that Satan must pay me back everything he stole from me, including interest. Proverbs 6:21 tells us: *"But if he is caught, he must pay back seven times what he stole, even if he has to sell everything in his house"* (nlt). Complacency, spiritual laziness, and a laissez-faire attitude—thinking that if Jesus wanted something to happen for you, He would just do it for you—must be dealt with in an urgent way. It is imperative that we partner with God, stand in alignment with our identity, and stand as the warriors we have been called to be, taking back what was stolen from us.

As co-heirs of Christ, we are promised far above our comprehension. In my thoughts concerning this concept, it seems like God takes those outlandish dreams of ours and uses them as a stepping-stone or a starting place to launch us into something much greater that we could not possibly imagine. If it is a dream that you could possibly tackle on your own, the dream is not big enough. God wants to show off big for you, for all to see, so that they know that He will do it for them, too. This may not be in the form of physical wealth, but in the priceless upgrade in your spiritual life. If we do not awaken to who God truly created us to be, we cannot fully war for our inheritance while on this earth.

Do not get me wrong: If you have invited Jesus to reside in you and you believe that He is your Lord and Savior, died for your sins, and defeated death by rising from the grave, then you are not going to lose your salvation. Salvation is not a passive process though. It is not only conquered via a simple salvation prayer. Satan is on the prowl with the ultimate plan to steal that from you. We must continually keep our eyes, faith, and trust in the Lord at all times. An incredible aspect about God that I am discovering is that there is *always* more to His presence, and I do not want to settle for anything less any longer. All I want is to have more of Him, and I want to continually learn more about His heart and His thoughts and will. A life filled and fueled by the Holy Spirit is one that is full of pure joy, regardless of what is going on. I want to be as close to the Father as possible, and if there is more, I want it. This is not necessarily representative of material things; although God is a wonderful Provider, that is not the point I am trying to make. Having more of His presence is all I could ever desire. If there is more to Him than what I have already experienced, then I want more of that. He does not need rich people in the church rolling around in the most expensive vehicles, most lavish homes, or private jets. I do not think that having wealth is bad-wealth is His!, God wants His children to prosper in everything, He is prosperity, but it is a matter of the heart. I believe that God wants to give you more beyond your wildest dreams so that you can fulfill your kingdom mandate.

How can you use your influence, finances, knowledge, or skills to share the love of Jesus? If your heart is aligned with the Father and the intentions of your heart are for Him and His mandate on your life, you have stepped into your identity in the army of God. Imagine then what repayment from the enemy would do for God's mission. It might not come to you in wealth or finances or in ways that your mind can fully comprehend, but being fully submitted to Him, His nature, and His ways will be a guide for you in how you can utilize what God has given and wants to give to you. God will always provide for your needs. I am not saying that God wants His children to live an impoverished life—actually the opposite. Second Corinthians 9:6–7 states: "*Whoever sows sparingly will also reap sparingly, and whoever sows generously will also reap generously. Each of you should give what you have decided in your heart to give, not reluctantly or under compulsion, for God loves a cheerful giver. And God is able to bless you abundantly, so that in all things at all times, having all that you need, you will abound in every good work*" (niv). We do have everything we need, and in many cases, we have an overabundance of what we actually need. We are to have the heart of a giver and to do everything with gladness, knowing that our needs will always be met.

There is always more in the Lord. This is true even if you have been a believer for your entire life and know full and well who you are in Christ, if you have deep intimacy and conversations with the Father. Even if you walk in miraculous signs and wonders, healing the sick, delivering people from demons, God is infinite in power and wisdom and your human mind cannot even begin to know all the ways of the Lord or His plans for you. This is where you should take His hand, getting out of His way, and submitting yourself to Him and saying, *"Lord, let it be so. Take the lead and I will follow."*

Activation

Think for a moment and write down your strengths and gifts. What are you really good at, or what have you done to hone a specific skill? Maybe it is a skill in your workplace. Maybe you are particularly gifted in computers or coding, art, music, writing, building, gardening, comprehension, teaching, or communication. There are infinite things that you could list here, but the point is to list something that brings fulfillment to your heart. It is something that brings you enjoyment, not something you are obligated to do or something that you dread doing.

After making that list, now write out the tragedies that you have gone though. What are the pivotal moments in your life that have been turning points for you? Ask the Lord to reveal how to connect the areas of your interest and gifting to the healing of your traumas. For me, I always loved to create and paint, but it was not really something that I focused on. It always was placed on the back burner as just a hobby, but the Lord told me that painting would bring healing to me and that it would be used to bring healing to others who have gone through trauma in their lives. How can the Lord use you with your desires and interests for the benefit of others?

SEATED IN VICTORY

The Promise

"When you go to war against your enemies and see horses and chariots and an army greater than yours, do not be afraid of them, because the Lord your God, who brought you up out of Egypt, will be with you. When you are about to go into battle, the priest shall come forward and address the army. He shall say: 'Hear, Israel: Today you are going into battle against your enemies. Do not be fainthearted or afraid; do not panic or be terrified by them. For the Lord your God is the one who goes with you to fight for you against your enemies to give you victory.'"

—Deuteronomy 20:1–4 NIV

We are not alone in any battle. The battles that rage on in our health, finances, relationships, work, and the atmospheres around us are ready to be fought by a big God if we just yield to Him, give Him our cares and worries (1 Pet. 5:7), and get out of His way and follow His lead. A yielded life is not a weak life, regardless of what others might think. I have heard it time and again that whenever a tragedy happens—a school shooting, a natural disaster, etc.—it will be posted or in a headline somewhere that prayers do nothing, that we need action. I do believe in action, but I also believe in prayer. Powerful prayers out of intercession and travail that rise to the throne room are some of the most powerful actions we can take. Submission to God and hearing from Him should absolutely be first in all things; then, of course, with His leading we can be mobilized to take physical action by donating our time, resources, and finances to assist those in need. Wimpy or "begging" prayers without authority will not get anything done. If you do not understand what communication with the Lord is and the power that it holds, then, of course, it will seem useless. We must stand firm, knowing who we are in Christ, taking our authority, and demanding the mountain to move. When you see something actually manifest right before your eyes as a result of your prayers, that builds incredible faith, and you will become unstoppable in what God has commissioned you to do.

Nothing can even come close to the power of God. It pains me that I lived most of my life asleep to the spiritual warrior inside of me. You might think that sounds arrogant, but it actually comes from humility and the knowledge that I am nothing without the Lord and it is not by my power or my will, but by the Lord's. Even though it pains me that I walked for the majority of my life in a spiritually sleep-like state, I also know that His timing is always perfect. I know that if I am yielded to God in divine alignment—fasting, praying, and seeking His face—and I step out in faith and take action, I cannot fail.

This is how you can live seated from victory. You can go into a situation, not out of fear, but out of celebration that the victory has already been won. Satan will throw counterattacks at you to attempt to derail you and the mission that you are on. We must always stay yielded to the move of God and what He wants to do and not be afraid, even when things only seem to be getting worse with our human eyes. This is part of walking in your inheritance and authority. Many have been taught that if they do not get up and get things done on their own, nothing will ever get done. I appreciate that concept to a point. God loves doers, people who are ready to take big leaps of faith. Sometimes God will give a directive and He is just waiting for us to take that big leap, but when we are stepping into battle or embarking on new territory, we may feel alone.

I urge you to ask the Lord to open your eyes to see the army around you battling on your behalf, and that you stay at the ready with your big step of faith. You have been given a promise and a directive. When you are faced with adversity, you can grip tightly to that anytime you feel all alone fighting a battle that seems impossible to be won. It says in Deuteronomy 31:6, *"Be strong and courageous. Do not be afraid or terrified because of them, for the Lord your God goes with you; he will never leave you or forsake you"* (niv).

You have been directed to be strong and courageous, to have no fear, along with the promise that the Lord goes with you and that He will *never* leave you. Having unshakable and radical faith is not an easy task, especially when our natural world is built upon fear. God knows that it is our first tendency to be afraid, and that is why He keeps reminding us not to be. Fear is a spirit that needs to be bound and cast away. When we take authority over the spirit of fear, then power, love, and a sound mind are loosed in our lives (2 Tim. 2:17). When you can intercede and pray from the spirit of power, the spirit of love, and the spirit of a sound mind, imagine what the Lord can do through you with prayer!

This makes me so excited for how powerful you are and you may not even realize it yet. Lean into what God is speaking to you right now. What has He put on your heart in your life right now? What are you fearing? I urge you to take authority over it right now and come at your situation seated from victory. Speak to the problem like it has already been defeated, even if it would need to take a miracle for that to happen. The Father God would love to give you your wildest dreams, and nothing is too far-fetched for Him if it is in alignment with His will. Bind any sprit of fear, repent for partnering with fear, and physically turn the opposite way. Loose power, love, and a sound mind over yourself, and speak to your mountain and tell it that it must move in the name of Jesus!

Growing up and going through school, I remember taking tests and being a little more skeptical of questions that had the option of "always" and "never" as answer options, because they are either seen as having no alternative or that it is an exaggeration. But when God says those words, we can stand on them, because He will always honor His Word and His promises, and He will deliver. Always.

Elisha and His Servant

I try to put myself in the middle of Bible stories and consider how I would have reacted in these moments. It is hard to imagine, because for most of us, these stories seem highly unlikely for the world that we live in, especially when we look at the Old Testament. What I have come to know is that these stories are still applicable to us if we seek their deeper meaning. The Word of God (the Bible) is alive and active, and the Lord wants to speak to you through its passages, even the Old Testament. Although we live under the new covenant, resulting from Jesus dying on the cross, we should not throw away the Old Testament. God never changes; He is the same yesterday, today, and tomorrow, yet He does new things.

Looking at the old covenant and the stories of the Old Testament as an opportunity to learn more about the character of God, we must ask Him to reveal Himself to us, filter the Old Testament stories through the cross, and accept His wisdom for today. The prophecies of the Old Testament are quoted many times in the New Testament, and I believe that it is important to understand all that the Lord wants to reveal to us.

The story of Elisha and the servant is chronicled in 2 Kings 6. (I prefer reading it in the New Living Translation.) I am going to tell this to you as a story, but be sure and read the story for yourself in your preferred version of the Bible (2 Kgs. 6:8–23).

Israel was under siege with the country of Aram, and the king of Aram relentlessly planned to win the war and overtake God's chosen people. This was no surprise, as throughout history, Israel had been attacked because of the promises the Lord had given to the Israelites. The king of Aram and his trusted officials met in their private chambers to plot to ambush the Israelite people. Along with his high-ranking officials, the king developed his strategies. The military leaders would direct their troops into the areas where the Israelites would be, but God had placed an advisor, a prophet close to the king of Israel.

The Lord gave Elisha, the prophet, the ability to supernaturally hear the voice of the king of Aram while he was making these plans against them. Elisha was not new to hearing the voice of the Lord or having the Lord use him to direct political matters. He had a great track record with hearing the voice of God, and he was then able to instruct the king of Israel that their military should avoid those specific locations, thus saving the soldiers' lives.

Of course, the king of Aram was not happy, and he immediately began to suspect that a traitor in his camp was telling his war secrets to the king of Israel. The men of Aram told their king that the prophet of the Lord, Elisha, was listening in on his plans on behalf of Israel. They then went and surrounded the city where Elisha was. Elisha's servant woke up and went outside his tent to see troops, chariots, and horses surrounding them. The Bible doesn't tell us how many troops had come against them—just that the city was surrounded—so you can imagine the fear that could arise in that moment when your life was endangered!

Immediately the servant was terrified, as I imagine anyone would be after witnessing such a thing without any revelatory knowledge from God. What would come to your mind in a moment like that? Many of us would probably believe that our time on earth was over at that point, just as the servant feared. He ran to get Elisha and cried out in panic, asking what they would do. Beyond the story telling us that he cried out, the following passage is my entire point. Elisha replied in verse 16: *"Don't be afraid! For there are more on our side than on theirs!"*

(nlt). Elisha knew something that the servant did not. He knew how this was going to go down; he knew they would not be harmed. The Lord was not going to allow them to be taken out in such a way. Elisha was approaching the situation from the standpoint of victory, and he had supernatural faith that allowed him to see what was to come.

What if we were able to see our battles in the same way? How would that change how we reacted to situations? *"Then Elisha prayed 'O Lord, open his eyes and let him see!' The Lord opened the young man's eyes, and when he looked up, he saw that the hillside around Elisha was filled with horses and chariots of fire"* (verse 17 nlt).

Elisha already knew the battle was won, but the servant did not. All he could see was his natural surroundings, and it appeared dreadful. They seemed defeated, and it felt like they were going to be overtaken. How on earth would they be able to defeat an army so great that it surrounded the city?

Elisha had a devoted relationship with God, and being consecrated and set apart in that relationship, God used him as a vessel to give revelatory knowledge and power for the sake of the many people whom God loved and was looking after, even if they did not chase after God in the same way. Elisha knew there were angel armies at the ready, just waiting for the decree to be spoken. He decreed that the enemy army of Aram would be blinded, and it was so. They then led the army to Samaria, where the king of Israel was, and asked that the eyes of the enemy army would be reopened. The king of Israel was just as confused in that moment, and he wondered what he was supposed to do with all of the people. He asked if he should lead them to be slaughtered, but Elisha told him no, that was not how he should treat prisoners of war. He was to feed them and allow them to return to where they had come from.

I presume that the enemy army had a radical encounter with the Lord that day. I imagine those men were never the same again. Their lives had been spared, and they were shown mercy by a loving God. This story concludes by telling us that after that, even the Arameans stayed away from the Israelites. Absolutely nothing can stop the move of God if He has put it into motion. Nothing can stop the plans God has for you. No form of oppression, no form of abuse, no loss, no bad situation, no battle, no war that has been assigned to stop you can prosper. When you stand in alignment with God and have eyes to see and ears to hear, nothing can stand in the way of that plan for you. Just as the angel armies were surrounding them at the ready, that still occurs for us today. What we see with our natural eyes is parallel to what is going on in the spirit that most of us are blinded to. Seek and ask the Lord to open your eyes to see the angels at the ready to battle on your behalf.

If for some reason you are met with death, there is no greater reward than to enter the kingdom of heaven and be freed from this troubled world in which you live. Standing on the promises of God does not mean that bad things will not ever happen to you; it just means that no matter what was meant to do you harm in any way, the Lord will always use it for good.

Many times we go through difficult seasons because of our own sin, or we take the wrong approach, fight back with our words or out of our flesh without seeking God, and we set our selves back from progression through our own faults. That still does not eliminate us from God's will for our lives. We must pick ourselves up, dust ourselves off, stand again, turn away from the old ways, repent and turn toward the face of the Lord, and say, "O Lord, open my eyes and let me see!"

Seated in Victory versus Fear of the Unknown

I am writing this chapter during a very interesting time in our own modern-day history. The spirit of COVID-19 has infiltrated the earth. Yes, I call it a "spirit" because I fully believe that it is a principality attack against the children of God (Eph. 6:12), and now more than ever, we need to be living from our victory. We need to apply the armor of God, stand in faith, and declare the Word of the Lord over the virus that has instilled fear into our land and the entire world.

I live about an hour north of Ground Zero of origin of the first case that was confirmed in the United States. Everything is shut down, schools are closed, all gatherings over ten people have ceased—including church gatherings—and fear is extremely high. Many people are worried about not being able to go to work, or they are worried about childcare if they have been deemed an essential worker. There is a looming fear of the unknown rising rapidly in everything I am seeing put out in the media and on all social media platforms. The people of God do know the end, and I have been praying that the Lord will open the church's eyes to see the legions of angels ready to fight at the decree that is declared by His people.

Everything meant for your harm, God will use for your good. I feel that through the nationwide/worldwide quarantines happening right now, the Lord wants to restore families and relationships. Revival first sparks in the hearts of families, and I believe we have an abundant opportunity to take back control of our family units at this time. We must repent of our evil ways and our reliance on other idols (media, sports, movies, entertainment), which in itself are not necessarily bad, but have replaced the presence and guidance of the Lord in our lives and family systems. With an outcome-mindedness, I am attacking this current problem from a place of victory. As we have been given this opportunity to be sheltered in place, I believe that my family will see healing like never before, and that our relationships and my marriage will be taken to a place that is dangerous to the kingdom of darkness. In a way, I feel like much of what I have walked through has prepared me for such a time as this, and God has been increasing my faith for this exact moment for the last three years. I know who is for me. I see who is fighting with me and who has gone before me. I see this virus as an attack from Satan, and the magnitude of this threat has been magnified and fueled by fear. They are saying it could take eighteen months before the threat is handled. I will prophesy right now that this virus will go out just as quickly as it came, as millions of God's sons and daughters rise to their warrior positions, travail, and sound the trumpets, and the false "crown" of this virus will fall, going back to the pit of hell where it came from.

This time hunkered in, however, will be used for our good and for our benefit. The enemy must pay back seven times what he has stolen, and we will live to see that repaid to our families like never before. The outpouring onto families will spill out into streets, neighborhoods, communities, cities, counties, regions, and nations. The outpouring of the Spirit of the Lord will come in with more ferocity and virility than the coronavirus has come in, and God's people will rise to meet the needs of the people in the community. There is a remnant rising up that is set apart, have been trained in the secret place, and do not cower to the enemy's attacks. They will take on new positions and have greater missions as they see people who need to feel the heart and the love of Jesus.

I see people upset that churches have closed their doors, but I actually feel excited for this, because the church isn't about a *building*—the *ecclesia*, or the real church, is the people. The Spirit of the Lord resides in His people, and He is not just for Sunday services. This is the church's opportunity to show the love of God like never before, pouring out His love and power even through the internet. This provides unbelievers who are not comfortable walking into a church building the opportunity to feel the love of God and hear the gospel in the comfort of their own homes. Imagine the reach that the church could have, doing this at a time when people are afraid and looking for peace. I am also excited about the small home gatherings that will spring up. Home churches that will host the presence of the Holy Spirit with radical obedience and see mighty moves of God breakthrough.

I decree Psalm 91:3–8 over you right now if you are reading this. The coronavirus pandemic might be over by the time of publication, but there is always something to hold fear about, right? So, I prophesy and declare this over your life right now in Jesus' name: He will rescue you from every hidden trap of the enemy, and He will protect you from any false accusation and any deadly curse. His massive arms are wrapped around you, protecting you. You can run under the covering of His majesty and hide. His arms of faithfulness are a shield, keeping you from harm. You will never worry about an attack of demonic forces at night nor have to fear a spirit of darkness coming against you by day. Do not fear a thing! Whether by night or by day, demonic danger will not trouble you, nor will the powers of evil that are launched against you. Even in a time of disaster, with thousands and thousands being killed, you will remain unscathed and unharmed. You will be a spectator as the wicked perish in judgment, for they will be paid back for what they have done!

THE
WILDERNESS SEASON

The Wilderness

Once my eyes were opened to the omnipresence of God in my everyday life, I was immediately placed into a transformative season that I will refer to as the "wilderness season." Everything that I held on to, the comforts on which I relied, the strongholds of anger and shame, all of it had to be dealt with. I believe that God uses wilderness seasons as times of reprieve and rest, as well as transformation and transition. He is so kind, and in order for complete transformation to occur, or for us to become a new creation, to obliterate all distractions and noise coming at us, and to make us fully reliant on the Lord, there needs to be a hiding season, away from everything that is competing for our attention. God wants us to come up higher in our thinking and in our actions, and I propose that He uses wilderness seasons as a launching pad to our upgrade.

I believe that we can intermittently put ourselves into wilderness seasons, which can be a great source for rest. I am often recharged by solitude, and I need to back away into seclusion when I am feeling bombarded, overwhelmed, or overstimulated. These are great times to humble ourselves before the Lord, to seek Him and get refilled, but real transformation occurs when we are placed in the wilderness by the Lord. How can we know the difference? If God placed us into a transformative period, our personal world, as we have known it, will be disrupted in some way that will seem inconvenient. All of a sudden, our normal routines will be disrupted, and we will be forced to seek refuge and hear God's voice to get through it.

This is a time for divine strategies, new ideas, new ways of thinking, and moving away from selfish desires. This was my experience in a God-led wilderness season. Everything in my life was shaken. The aspects that were not of God had to pass away; some relationships faded away, and new ones sprouted. While individual components of this time were hard to process and understand, like the fading away of people in my life, it was a great opportunity to be near the heavenly Father. It was not painful or destitute or free from comforts—like a literal "wilderness"—it was not barren or a dry place. It was an internal wilderness, and I could feel old ways passing away, being stripped away, and new ways being rejuvenated into something beautiful. It was like watching beauty spring from ashes. I fed on the living Word of God; He gave me a prayer language; He opened my eyes to see His goodness and mercy; He showed me His nature; and He removed people from my life who could no longer be present. Not that they were bad relationships per se, but they were not going to help me progress in the growth that God had intended for me, so they had to be pushed aside. It was painful in a lot of ways as well, sort of like the birthing process is. Child labor in the natural is a lot like laboring in the spirit. There are waves of pressure that arise, crushing you on all sides and what is produced is from the Lord. Do not give up when it is hard and the pressure is coming on strong from all sides, seek the Lord and lean into it.

Through this time, God showed me how much He loves me and what He wanted to do through me. Each day He gave me a new promise to hold on to, and He addressed every fear, doubt, and obstacle in my thinking that was hindering me from hearing His voice and His plan. This time was not all sunshine and rainbows, however. It was similar to a rigorous bootcamp, a spiritual bootcamp if you will. It was hard work because I had to be willing to see myself through the eyes of Jesus and come to the realization that there was a huge gap between me and Him.

Our goodness does not come anywhere close to His goodness, and we are so unworthy of His mercy when we see Him in His glory. The wilderness creates an atmosphere that is filled with strong conviction, in which you are very clear on your ways that are sinful. The consecrated place of the wilderness does not warrant our evil tendencies. I was strongly convicted of a sin of mine that most of my closest confidantes had told me was not a big deal. In all honesty, when you look at it through the human eye lens, it really was not a big deal. I was not hurting anyone, and I am only human after all.

I could have made that argument, and that was the argument that was presented to me, but that was not the conviction I was receiving from the Lord. He was very clear with me that that was not His way and that it must go in order for me to move forward. When you are in His presence and the fear of the Lord comes upon you in a mighty way, everything that He highlights to you is crystal clear. There is no question, and in that moment, I knew that it was no longer okay to partner and to excuse certain ways of living as just being human. We are human, and we are sinners, and we will always be torn in a constant struggle between the flesh and the spirit.

I am not saying that I have been made perfect. The closer I get to God, the more I realize the separation between us. This comes from a more humbled place of knowing that I am fully loved by a good Father, but I am not His equal. I am a sinner and I need a Savior, but this relentless battle is not mine alone. I have a Partner and an Advocate to walk alongside me on this journey, and I am so humbled by that. He loves little ol' me, with all my flaws, cracks, crevices, and bad choices that I make each and every day. He is the Potter, and I am the clay. He continually restores my broken places as I submit and consecrate myself to Him.

In moments when I miss the mark, He still loves me, and He says, *"My darling daughter, that is not who you are. Come up higher with Me."* He will never stop saying that, and He will never leave me, no matter how badly I mess up, but He *will* correct me, and sometimes that has to be done in the quiet, secret place with Him alone.

I still go back to that old way often, but that specific area that He highlighted to me is something that I get an immediate check in my spirit on. It has raised a level of discernment in me when I see others doing that same thing, and it allows me to intercede on their behalf because God wants us to be helping others through the things from which we ourselves have been delivered. I have spoken about the fear of the Lord through this book, but friend, I need to emphasize that we should all be seeking to experience that. The consecration, wisdom, and knowledge that comes from fearing Him (like I have described before, it is not "being afraid" of Him, but having a reverent fear of His might, trembling in His presence and fearing His absence or Him telling you He never knew you, which is His wrath) is the launching pad to greater things. When you lean in, turn from your physical ways of working in the world, and seek His face, nothing else matters. He can do exponential feats through you, because you are consecrated to Him.

We are all human and are not in any way perfect, but that is what I love about seeing God move through people—especially if they are an unlikely person whom you would think God would never use. God loves to show off through unexpected and uncommon people, so that when God's glory moves, there is no doubt that it is the hand and move of God at work and not human might or will. I perceive that individuals may think similar things about me. My mistakes in this life could warrant doubt among people who do not like me. I am so excited for what God has shown me that He will do through me in the future. This requires a place of humble reverence for the Lord and for me to continually empty myself of my selfish ambition.

God wants to do the same for you. No one is too far gone from His will that He cannot heal them, restore them, and use them as a disciple for His mission. We must be careful about whom we judge or take offense at. God loves everyone, just as He loves you, with your faults and all. No matter what your personal opinions and judgments about a person are, you are not fit to judge the matters of the heart. We must continue to seek the Lord in what He is doing and saying in every area of our lives, and continue to be unoffended at what He wants to do in us and through us.

Growing Closer to His Heart

"Remember how the Lord your God led you through the wilderness for these forty years, humbling you and testing you to prove your character, and to find out whether or not you would obey his commands."

—DEUTERONOMY 8:2 NLT

Israel was rescued out of Egypt from severe oppression and slavery. They had received the promise of a land of prosperity and all that they could imagine waiting for them, but they had to go through a wilderness season first. Why? God uses wilderness seasons to refine us, to obliterate thoughts and ways that are not shaped in His image. They needed to understand that they were no longer slaves, and they needed to step into their warrior destiny and enter into the love of the Father. Instead, they doubted, and they grew weary of all they had to do. Some wanted to return to the abusive slavery situation that they had just came out of, because it was familiar.

I think that is where many of us have rejected such refining seasons as "not of God" and rebuked them as if they were from Satan, because they did not feel good or they were not comfortable. If I have learned anything about my relationship with God, it is that He is always asking me to take a leap of faith and risk looking like a crazy person. His ways are not our ways or the world's ways, and we could be mocked and ridiculed for taking a step out in faith. We are not promised a simple, comfortable life, no matter how much we strive for that. The reward that awaits our obedience is far greater than anything in this lifetime can reward us for. Christians have been hiding in this world, or trying to become part of the world, for a long time. Initially, I think that our hearts were right; the intention was to reach people who had never sought the Lord before so that people could feel the love of God, but the thin line has been blurred in changing the narrative and omitting portions of the Bible so as to not offend anyone. I believe that God does not want people hiding and professing their faith and proclaiming His Word and the hope that it brings only on Sundays. He wants for us to be equipped to be sent out into all areas of our influence—whether that be our work, schools, politics, community, or the nations. Missions is for your community and workplace as well as going on a mission trip to Africa or some other foreign nation. Our lives are to be living and breathing missions of God so that everyone we come into contact with will want to draw near because there is something different about us.

You hold the light of Jesus Christ in you, but for some people, that light has been dimmed in order to not make others feel uncomfortable. When God shines His light on sin, it does not feel comfortable, but the other side is the restoration and healing power of His love and grace. I have a feeling that the Lord is drawing a line in the sand on many aspects of our lives, but especially for Christians and the church. There is no conforming, and there must be a wilderness season that looks out of control, and maybe looks a little messy, to help refine what really matters. We must get our hearts aligned with God again so that the Bride, the church, can rise to give people truth in love, hope without conforming, and peace without backing down or hiding.

Are we humble enough to be convicted of our wrongs as the collective body of Christ and own the ways in which we have failed? Will we allow the Lord to mold and shape our hearts to be more like this and continually test us, even if we continue to fail? Will we obey His commands and serve with a kingdom and a victory mindset, or will we live in fear and never enter into the promised land that He has provided? If you are a follower of Christ, you are a part of the body, and each part is integral to the mission of God. It will take all of us to awaken to our purpose and mandate, to work as a collective body to fulfill it.

Now is the time to humble ourselves and turn from every wicked way in which we knowingly or unknowingly participated. We need to repent for the systems of religion with which we have partnered over having a cherished relationship with the Father, and we must turn in the opposite direction toward where God is going. We need to have keen discernment for the times and the seasons, and He will hear our prayers and heal our land.

God uses wilderness seasons because He loves us, and He knows how destructive we are to ourselves and situations when we are not walking in alignment with Him. If we want to see heaven come to earth, then we must learn more about His ways. Jesus was very offensive to the religious crowd who studied the coming Messiah in the biblical texts and teachings, but they did not discern when He showed up face-to-face with them. We cannot merely just memorize the Bible. We must encounter the Holy Spirit who lives in the active Word of God. I do not want to miss a move of God because I was too hardhearted, cynical, or skeptical of what He was doing, and I discredit it for a lack of discernment. That level of discernment only happens when we are eagerly seeking His face.

Highlight Your Blessings

What area are you being hit the hardest with right now in your trials? For me, it has been my voice. I felt like I was being silenced in some way. Anytime I used my voice, I felt so much shame and ridicule. I had used my voice in nonconstructive ways, and this became an open door for Satan to use against me each time I attempted to use my voice. I used my words as weapons—and not in the way the Lord intended. I spoke harshly to the people whom I loved the most. Satan used that as an area of condemnation, continually accusing me of my past and making me believe that was who I was.

The tactic of the enemy is to use a mistake or a sin and make you believe that is your identity, then embed into you the thought that you are what you do. I believe the Lord used this time as well to make me see what ways in which I was walking that were not His will for me. As I have mentioned a few times, the Lord corrects and convicts us to teach us that our ways are not His ways, but He will always do this in love, with the promise of hope for the future. God's loving mercy said to me, *"Using your voice to hurt people is not what I have called you to do. This is not who you are or what I made you for. Come with Me—come up higher. Rise above the old way, which has already passed away. Come up higher with Me, and I will use your voice to bless the nations."*

What a promise! In my wilderness season, which lasted about a year, the Lord spoke a new promise over me every day. Some of these promises are so outlandish that it seems highly unlikely that they would ever come to pass and it is clear that they cannot come to pass in my own strength. The wildest and most abundant dreams that we can see for ourselves do not even compare to what God wants to do with us and through us that will utterly baffle us and everyone around us. He wants to create something *with* us that is so wildly beautiful and powerful that will reveal His nature and glory.

God loves to show off for His children, for the purpose of bringing attention to His love for everyone. He wants to give you abundant blessings so that you can elevate and bless others. It is all for building the kingdom. So, if your intentions are selfish in nature, or you seek fame and wealth to collect goods and prizes, then you are not ready to carry what God intends for you. The statement, "God will not give you more than you can handle," sounds nice, and I can see how someone would say that to comfort another who is going through a difficult time. While there is no verse that directly says that, I would like to propose a different spin on this saying. We are told that we can do nothing apart from His strength, so on the one hand I believe this saying implies that there is nothing too hard or difficult for God and that we can seek Him in the most dire of times for strength, courage, and wisdom. We also know that the Lord does not ever send us anything to harm us. He doesn't send evil or disaster to us, so if we are facing cataclysmic events or issues, we must remember that He is bigger than anything that we face, and we can always lean on Him. What we cannot handle in our own will and actions is an opportunity to seek the Lord to step in with His mighty power. Dreadful things happen in this life, and sometimes it feels like they come in crashing waves of defeat, loss, death, burdens, and hurts. There is an invitation here to turn toward Him and say to Him, "Lord, I need Your help. I need Your hand to step in here and give me protection, rest, and healing."

While all of that is true, I suggest that this saying is not about tests and trials. God wants us to be fully reliant on Him and His power. I believe that this saying could be referring to the weight of His glory—or the mantle, assignment, and anointing He has for us to carry in this world. If we are broken, walking in sin without repentance, not growing in relationship with Him, or not seeking Him in all things—if He put that weight on our shoulders before we were fully prepared, before going through the bootcamp to strengthen and condition our spiritual muscles—understanding our identity and calling, the weight would crush us. We would fall—and not just physically. We could do more damage than good for other believers if we were to pick up the mantle before we are ready.

So, God continues to test us, to see how we respond in certain situations. If we fail, He will always give us another opportunity. We are going to fail and miss it, and He already knows that. I sense that He enjoys this process with us because He already knows how we will walk through it all. He sees us on the other side with victory, and I can picture Him cheering us all on to come up higher. When we are ready to bear the weight of His glory, there is another opportunity for us to learn how to navigate through it and turn toward the Father. His yoke is easy and burden is light (Matt. 11:30) even through the weightiness of His glory compared to the weight of the world. We will not be complete in Christ until His return, so each day is a moment for us to conquer and become all that He intended for us to be.

God will highlight the areas of our weakness, the areas where we have messed up the greatest, or the areas where we have been attacked the hardest, to use them for our good and for the good of others. If you have been in an abusive situation, that was not God's will nor His intention. He is saying, "Come up with Me. Rise up, and I will heal you and use you to be a rescue and a hope to others who have suffered the same." All for His Glory.

Upgrade Season

When we are met with condemnation from the enemy, and he is recounting all our faults and all the wrongs that we have done, in our shame about our wrongs, we succumb to the thought that he is completely right. I am not saying that we should be walking around doing wrong because our sins will be written off. Living a life of repentance is a constant way of life. We must seek to make right the wrongs that we do. God made a way for us to take accountability for our actions, turn away from that way of life (called repentance), and walk in the opposite direction toward Him. God will always walk in the opposite direction from Satan. When Satan comes to bring shame, God will come in and speak victory. When Satan tells us that we are nobodies, God will call us saints. When Satan calls us liars, God will give us a megaphone. You see? God is not in the business of using our wrongs against us; our continual rehashing and seeking forgiveness for something we are feeling condemnation over is not God's way, nor is it His will for us. He holds no accounts of our wrongs if we live in repentance, humble ourselves, and turn from our evil ways. He has already washed us white as snow by the blood shed on the cross.

If you have been feeling shame and you experience that break off of you with the encounter of freedom, that is an upgrade in the spirit. Every attack from the enemy carries an upgrade. The reward is perseverance, being complete and whole in His eyes and lacking nothing (James 1:2–4). Every trial you face has an upgrade attached to it, just waiting for you to reach out and grab it. In my experience, I have never received freedom from something that I was not first made aware of. If I were wrapped in sin, it would be revealed so that I could repent and receive freedom. If I were under attack, revelation would come to me through submission to the Father in seeking His wisdom. It does not just come to you randomly. You must be working toward becoming more like Jesus every day, and every situation, good or bad, gives you an opportunity to have a response and be in communication with the Lord, who is mighty to save and mighty to bless His children. He aches for you to seek Him; He wants to show you amazing things. He wants to instill creativity in you and help you to create something with Him to help others get set free. He is not bound or restrained by limitations, and He can accelerate you to catch you up to where He needs you to be.

I never thought that I would write a book; writing was never something that I would claim as something I enjoyed. The Lord had me writing down what I was hearing from Him and testing it for three years. He was training me in something new and it was by His grace alone that this has come to fruition. God convicted me my old ways of believing what I am not and invited me to follow Him into something new. By doing so and giving Him my yes, living in repentance and being open to what He wanted to say to me, He gave me all that I needed to complete what He wanted me to complete. It is all Him—hallelujah! All glory and honor goes to Him. Where I was speaking angry words and hostility, He had me write words of peace. He had me painting to bring healing to the hearts of His wounded daughters who also hold shame for what they have done or what has been done to them. This is an invitation to come under the shelter of His wings and feel His love, glory, mercy, truth, peace, and healing; to discover what He wants to do through you for His glory.

Can You Carry It?

I pray that you are hopeful for your future after reading this chapter. We never "arrive" or come to all knowledge until we get to heaven. Even the greatest generals in the faith have to continually work on their progress and personal journeys with the Lord. Every upgrade comes with learning how to navigate, to hear and see what God wants to do in that time. What are you currently carrying? What are the areas in your life that God is highlighting to you where He wants to bring blessing to you in this next season? What are some ways that you can change your response to how you have been responding to circumstances around you? Do you need to respond with more love, joy, peace, patience, kindness, goodness, faithfulness, gentleness, or self-control? There are rewards on the other side of walking in His fruit. You may see restoration in relationships, an unexpected promotion at work might come along, your response to your children will improve, or you might all of a sudden make new friends who are walking through similar situations. (Hint: This is an area for you to bring blessing to them and for them to bless you as well.) These are God interventions of blessings upon your life. He cares about every small or minute detail of your life, as well as all the big happenings that occur. It is so fun to catalogue these blessings each day. If you are finding it difficult to see how the Lord is working in your life, one simple step would be to start journaling what you are grateful for, the new or changed events that occurred in your day that seem out of the norm in a positive way. Looking back over those details will string together a beautiful picture of just how wonderful God intervenes in your everyday life. Recognizing where He is showing up for you or trying to get your attention will further increase your heart posture toward Him and allow you to hear Him more expectantly. When I wake up in the morning, my prayer is always of one of expectation. *What do You want to do today, Lord?* He responds to His language, and when we operate from our heavenly seat and respond with a kingdom-type response instead of a fleshly response of inconvenience, we open ourselves to greater wisdom and intimacy with the Father.

God ultimately cares about the intentions of the heart and our character, not so much our deeds. Our actions mean nothing to Him unless we are in submission to Him and His will. Do not mistake my urgency to take action for God as a way to gain more favor in the eyes of the Lord. We do not enter His gates by our deeds; our salvation rests only on believing in Jesus. We cannot be saved by deeds and actions alone. By living a fully submitted life to God and asking Him to continually search our hearts and intentions and to build in us character, the outcome and the fruit displayed is going to result in some sort of action to build His kingdom from a place of service and yield versus from a place of selfishness and determining personal gain.

It says in Jeremiah 17:10, "*I the Lord search the heart and examine the mind, to reward each person according to their conduct, according to what their deeds deserve*" (niv). It is all about the heart and what flows through it and what we are being fed by. This includes the music we are listening to, the opinions of others we are clinging to, or the movies we watch. Everything flows through the gates of our hearts, and we must be vigilantly aware of the effects outside sources of information have and determine our ways when we are instructed to seek the Lord with all our hearts and minds. When we are more mindful of these areas, we are more aware of His ways, and out of our bellies can flow rivers of living water.

Devotional

Above all else, guard your heart, for everything you do flows from it. Keep your mouth free of perversity; keep corrupt talk far from your lips. Let your eyes look straight ahead; fix your gaze directly before you. Give careful thought to the paths for your feet and be steadfast in all your ways. Do not turn to the right or the left; keep your foot from evil.

— PROVERBS 4:23–27 *NIV*

Remember that the Lord does not condemn. He brings revelation so that we can seek a deeper relationship with Him and turn from ways in which we have knowingly and unknowingly participated in creating greater separation between ourselves and the Father. Sit for a moment with your eyes closed and ask the Holy Spirit to reveal the things that He has for you. No matter how outlandish they seem, write them down. They could come to you in a picture, be represented in a feeling, or enter your mind as a word. Be open to hearing from your loving Father.

_____

_____

_____

Now write down a few things that you can drop and set aside (paths or ways) that are destructive to you reaching that place that the Lord revealed to you. What areas in your life are in the way of what you sensed Him say to you above, that would prevent it from coming to fruition?

_____

_____

_____

Now take some time and repent of partnering with ways that would hinder you from drawing closer in relationship with the Father, or that would hinder you from completing what He has for you. Not all things that He shows us are necessarily evil, but anything that becomes elevated above the Lord is an idol. Ask Him to reveal to you your next steps and how you can draw near and walk on the path He has for you. It could be to tithe or sow into a work of God's through another person or ministry; to pray more; to surround yourself with spiritual advisors; or to take a leap of faith and ask someone if you could pray for them. Other ways that God could ask you to be obedient include to fast or to take communion. Whatever the Lord shows you, write it down. It is not limited to the ways I listed.

_____

_____

_____

"A good man brings good things out of the good stored up in his heart, and an evil man brings evil things out of the evil stored up in his heart. For the mouth speaks what the heart is full of."

—LUKE 6:45 NIV

My flesh and my heart may fail, but God is the strength of my heart and my portion forever.

—PSALM 73:26 NIV

We have a God who loves us beyond comprehension, and He desires for us to be successful and walking fully in His ways. He will not leave or forsake us, and He will always reach down, grab our hand, and stand us up again, giving us the opportunity to try again. Our flesh and our hearts may fail, and we have already fallen short, but He raises us up in His ways, and shapes and molds our characters to walk with hearts of love. We have the perfect Person in Jesus to show us the way of living. I would love to pray for you now.

Heavenly Father,

Thank You for Your tender heart for all Your children, especially your daughters who read this book. I pray that Your Spirit of Revelation will come upon them now and reveal Your heart and love for them at this time. I pray that as they give You their past, worries, cares, shame, doubts, and sins, You will renew them and speak new life into them. You are mighty to save, and You are a good, good Father. I pray blessings to fall upon everyone reading this book. I pray that Your mercy and love will cover all things and that they would be made white as snow by Jesus' blood. Thank You for Your desire for us to know You intimately. In Jesus' name I pray, amen.

ADORED

You Are God's Beloved

"Put me like a seal over your heart, like a seal on your arm. For love is as strong as death, jealousy is as severe as Sheol; its flashes are flashes of fire, the very flame of the Lord. Many waters cannot quench my love, nor will rivers overflow it; if a man were to give all the riches of his house for love, it would be utterly despised."

— SONG OF SOLOMON 8:14 NASB

We love Him because He first loved us.

— 1 JOHN 4:19 NIV

There is no adequate way to fully comprehend the love that God has for us. It is so big and all-consuming. You cannot hide from it, and He is always searching and seeking you and your heart. When we go through tumultuous times or traumatic events and feel absolutely broken in mind, heart, body, and spirit, it gives room for the Lord to do what He has always wanted to do. I believe this is because our defense mechanisms are down during times such as these. We are vulnerable to outside attack, but we are also open and willing for "something" to rescue us out of a place of desperation, even if we have fortress walls built up around our heart for protection and self-defense. Moments of despair or last-ditch efforts cause individuals to seek and test if there is truly a living God who is tangible in moments of need and beyond. The Lord loves to reveal Himself, and He wants to reveal Himself to you today. I get the sense that God wants to restore His daughters who have fought long and hard battles that have caused emotional, physical, and spiritual trauma. Having been in this place myself, I know what it feels like for the chains to break, the weight to lift, the fog to clear, and the prison doors to go flying open. There is nothing like the freedom found in Christ Jesus. In my experience in over thirty-three years as a follower of Jesus and a churchgoer, I was never really taught to hear the voice of God or what it really meant to be a daughter of Christ. We have become over-reliant on the church to feed us spiritually without taking personal responsibility for our own spiritual needs. I completely take responsibility for my immature spiritual ways, my rebellious years, and the walls that I built up around my heart from past hurts. Our salvation is not in the hands of a spiritual leader—it is a personal walk and journey with the Lord—but how do we practically learn to hear the voice of God, especially if they are not preaching the entire Gospel? If the church spent more time on getting people acquainted with how He speaks, how He moves, and the different ways He loves to encounter us, we would have more mature people of faith in the church who could help others on their personal journey. And that would in turn take some pressure off the church leadership.

I do not mean to offend anyone with these observations, but it is not a secret how badly churches are hurting right now. Pastors are walking away from the faith, and churches are closing their doors at a rapid rate. There must be something more and deeper to teaching intimate relationships with our heavenly Father than just motivational messages on Sundays. People want depth, and in troubling times, they want to encounter a big God and experience the promises that are preached week in and week out.

How do you learn to do life with Jesus? What does it look like to be fully dependent and empowered by the Holy Spirit? The power that raised Jesus from the dead is the power that lives in each and every one of us who have given our lives to Christ. We were not meant to live mediocre lives or to just go through the motions and get through the day. I am hungry and thirsty for all that He has to offer me. Why? Because He saved me from death, and I watched Him breathe life back into my baby. He redeemed me, forgave me, and showed me that He was the one person who would never leave me. He would never fall out of love with me. I could never make Him love me less or make Him change His mind about me.

This was not the same God I was taught about growing up—a violent God that I could never be good enough to encounter. Instead of having a healthy fear of the Lord, I was simply afraid of Him. He is a roaring Lion, but He is also a lamb and we need to know Him as both. Learning only about the wrath of the Lord brings unhealthy fear without relationship and conversely, only learning about the lamb that Jesus is breeds a life without accountability. He is just as much the God in Genesis as much as He is the God in Revelations. The fear of the Lord rests in knowing what happens when God is not with you. It is not a happy ending to have God absent or to not have the Spirit of God residing inside of you. This is an eternal decision that we all have to make and we cannot hide from the parts of the Bible that make us uncomfortable any longer. There is hope because this gift is free, but we must open our hearts to the totality of who Jesus is and begin to emotionally wrestle with the scriptures that we do not understand. It is time for the churches to preach the entirety of who the Godhead is.

As I was walking through this transformation and getting on the other side into deeper revelations of the Father's heart and the love and adoration that He feels for His people, I have encountered many wonderful daughters of Christ who feel the same way—who were not taught how to walk in daily communion with the Lord in a practical or tangible way. I realize that our journey and walk with the Lord cannot be put into a box or become a one-size-fits-all approach to teach people how to have a relationship with the Lord, but it would be wonderful to see more and more sons and daughters stepping outside of a theological box and grabbing what the Lord has prepared for us at the table.

As I prayed about this, I felt there were a few practical and tangible aspects that we could all do to get the ball rolling. First, just like with any relationship, especially an intimate relationship, it develops more deeply over time. From a practical aspect, I communicate with my husband about our day and any decisions that need to be made. I submit to his leadership as the head of our household, not because he is my keeper or because he rules over me, but because he is my partner and confidante, and it is the biblical order of the household. We make decisions together, big and small. Just as married people would submit to each other, we (followers of Christ) are the Bride of Christ, and He wants us to partner with Him daily to be in fellowship and ask what He thinks about all aspects of our lives.

What does it look like to walk with Jesus and never let go of His hand? This can encompass many facets of our daily living. We live in a fast-paced, technologically savvy world, and we are constantly on the go. Busyness is a direct threat to intimacy in any relationship, including our relationship with the Lord. Spending a few moments with Him when we wake up, when we bless our meals, and at bedtime is lovely, but it is not enough. We must be fully submitted in heart, mind, will, and emotions, at all times. Satan devotes 168 hours a week to steal, kill, and destroy everything good from our lives. He will attack our self-worth, self-image, relationships, marriages, thoughts, actions, and reactions. He uses rejection as a deep wound that brings about pride, rebellion, insecurity, shame, guilt, condemnation, and fear—

among many others—to set up defense mechanisms and to build walls around the areas God has planned for us.

We must learn how to get into the secret place with him, put away all distractions, and fully submit and be willingly trained by the Godhead in that space. As you do that, it becomes easier to know how to commune with the Lord throughout the day. If you are thinking that reading this is overwhelming because you just cannot fit one more thing into your schedule, then my dear, dear friend—you must rearrange your priorities. This is an urgent matter, and we all must change as soon as possible. This will not look the same for everyone. The way one person hears God will differ from others, and God made our personalities so wonderfully unique and brilliant that He wants to partner with us through every part of our day. Start your day with asking the Lord what He wants to do today and how you can help Him. Then as you move through your day, ask the Lord what He is doing in that moment. As we grow in discernment of who He is, we learn to recognize Him in various ways. Another way to dive into a deeper daily walk with Jesus is to ask the Holy Spirit for help of all kinds of ways. In Isaiah 41, it mentions over and over again how much the Lord wants to help us. He wants to help us so that we will then want to help others in return. *"If you are having trouble with your car, I can help,"* says the Lord. *"I hear your cries for help, and help is on the way."*

I get very emotional reading Isaiah 41 in the Bible. A pastor spoke that chapter over me that he felt the Lord had on His heart for me, and he instructed me to read it and keep reading it. Every time I read it, a new key message from the scripture stands out at me. The key concept I realized the Lord was speaking to me was, *"Missy, can you ask for more help? I want to help. I have sent you help, and you turned it away. Yield and accept My help."* I have always been independent growing up and it was an area of pride that needed to be dismantled in my heart. It was preventing me from growing closer to the Father and hearing His voice, and it was hindering every relationship I had.

Even if you cannot physically see anything happening, He is always at work in you, for you, and through you if you allow Him. Are you willing to be a participant in your healing? Are you ready to grow deeper in love with the Creator of your heart, who knows how many hairs are on your head?

Knowing your identity in Christ not only gives you authority, but it ultimately gives you intimacy with the Lord. Without intimacy and relationship with the Father, there is no authority on which to stand. Authority in the name of Jesus only comes from submission and a walk with the Lord; it is not by our will or our power. So, if Jesus lives in us, it is His will and His power, and then it is His authority. We get the pleasure of being in a relationship with the Creator of the universe, and we allow Him to work through us to help other people. God put Jesus in you—the One with whom He is well pleased, His beloved Son. You are a co-heir with Jesus, and God looks at you the same way that He looks at Jesus.

When I was in the midst of my turmoil, I mentioned before that I made a lot of mistakes using my words to hurt people. None of this was intentional—it just sort of bubbled out of me when I felt like I was being pushed into a corner. I believe that these character flaws have always been a part of me, but either they were suppressed, or I was able to control them. The Lord has a way of revealing or convicting us of areas of our lives in which we are walking or things we are holding on to that are not from Him. He told me in my prayer time that I would not progress until I gave those over to Him. Anger, resentment, and negativity were not allowed to follow me into my next season because for what I was to carry, the extra negative weight would break me. You see, He loves me so much that He would not give me more than I could carry. He wanted to see me whole, because there was more for me on the other side of all of that. If He would do that for me, then He absolutely wants to do that for you, too.

At the same time as I was going through this character refinement period, the Lord was also revealing to me relationships that could not continue. I was not adored by many during this time in my life for many different reasons—some from my own actions and some not. I would not even say that I adored myself, either. One day I came across a jewelry company that made "prophetic" jewelry: After selecting the style of jewelry you wanted, you provided your name, and the people at the company would pray over you and then send you that piece of jewelry with an engraving of what they felt was on the Father's heart for you in that moment. When I received my necklace, it was engraved with the word *ADORED*. It also had a note that said: "Beloved, you are sought after and adored by your heavenly Father. Jesus is madly and crazy in love with you. He did everything possible to close any gap between you and Him. He gave you this life because He loves you. You cannot change His affection for you; it is eternal and unchanging. He is with you always, and He will always be faithful to you." I have to tell you, I felt so awkward wearing this necklace that said "adored" for everyone to see. I actually felt shame about this, because I knew that many people really disliked me and were gossiping and plotting behind my back. Wearing this necklace felt like a scarlet letter to me at first, but as I continued to wear it, I felt God was telling me as I went through my day everything He loved about me. He was prophesying my identity over me. Of course, He knew what was going on around me and the pain and heartache I was feeling. But He was calling me up higher, to live from my heavenly seat as His adored daughter. He was moving me in the opposite direction from the path where I was headed. He was saying, *"Darling daughter, I have so much more for you, but you have to come up here to get it."* When I say that I cannot get over the loving-kindness of the Father, I mean it. No one has ever spoken to me in my darkest moments with so much love, encouragement, hope, and promise. I doubted if what I was hearing was actually from Him or if it was just me. But I have learned to hear His voice, because He commonly speaks to me as random thoughts that are not like my normal thoughts. When this happens, I get my journal out and I start writing. Over time I was able to distinguish what was likely coming from me and what I felt was from the Lord. The Lord will always confirm what He says and for me, He does that through scripture, encounters and conversations with other people, or sometimes I will see a word He gave me on a street sign or a billboard picture. These confirmations are an invitation to go deeper and receive more revelation.

Activation

If you are wanting to grow in learning how to hear the Lord's voice, here is a simple exercise that you can do. Find fifteen minutes in which you can be alone without interruption. Set a timer for five minutes. You will end up repeating the timer three times. For the first five minutes, pray without stopping. If you have a prayer language, pray in your special heavenly prayer language, or in tongues. If you do not have a prayer language, simply pray in your native tongue and just speak to the Lord what is on your heart. Tell Him everything you love about Him. Thank Him for what He has done for you and your family. Ask Him to encounter you in a new way. Ask Him for a fresh filling of His Spirit and ask Him to give you a prayer language. Speak to Him whatever you feel comfortable saying. After the timer goes off, restart it, and then sit quietly with a journal or something else to write on. Just sit peacefully and listen to what God is telling you. Write everything down that comes into your mind during this time. Do not fear getting anything wrong—it is important to be able to distinguish what are our own thoughts and what are from God. Make sure you are in a quiet place, and if you need to do a brain dump of everything floating around in your head, do that first before you even start. We need to get away from all our distractions and declutter our brains before we can hear His whisper. Then, for the final five minutes, read your Bible. You can do this on a digital application, but I prefer to do this with an actual Bible in hand. I usually ask the Lord for a passage of Scripture to read, but if I am not sensing anything specific, then I will just open the Word and start reading wherever I land; then I read without stopping for five minutes.

What this simple exercise has done for me is that by praying, giving thanks, and asking for God's presence, I am inviting Him to speak to me. I am inviting Him to open my ears and my heart to hear His voice. By writing down everything that comes to mind, I am able to look back and see a difference in who the speaker was.

And by reading through the Scriptures, I am further inviting the Lord to speak to me through His written Word. Oftentimes, I get a confirmation through the passage about what had popped into my mind earlier and what I wrote down in my journal. Those moments never get old—those absolute times of confirmation that God hears me, speaks to me, and I have the ability to hear His voice.

You do not need to be a minister or a pastor to be able to hear the voice of God. You were created for a relationship with the Father, to hear from Him. I believe that we are in a time right now when the Lord wants to pour out His Spirit to all of us, just like in the book of Acts, so that we can be a source of hope and light in a dark world.

Bless Those Who Curse You

"But I say to you who hear, love your enemies, do good to those who hate you, bless those who curse you, pray for those who mistreat you. Whoever hits you on the cheek, offer him the other also; and whoever takes away your coat, do not withhold your shirt from him either. Give to everyone who asks of you, and whoever takes away what is yours, do not demand it back. Treat others the same way you want them to treat you."

—Luke 6:27–31 NASB

Then Peter came and said to Him, "Lord, how often shall my brother sin against me and I forgive him? Up to seven times?" Jesus said to him, "I do not say to you, up to seven times, but up to seventy times seven."

—Matthew 18:21–22 NASB

I pray that your heart is open to hearing the heart of the Lord on this matter. I do not come at this with criticism, and I do not discredit your story or any hardships that you may have faced. I had to wrestle with what the Lord was speaking to me on this topic, not because I did not agree with what He was saying, but because of how incredibly difficult—even impossible—this is to do in our own power. Jesus was betrayed, beaten, wounded, harassed, abused, spit upon, ridiculed, and ripped to shreds in death for our iniquities. I thank the Lord of Hosts as I sit and write that His wounds heal us of all things. He paid for our healing. He is for us, and He loves us beyond measure. We are never alone, and anything that has been done to you will one day be vindicated by the Lord—even if it is not in this lifetime.

We have all been wronged or sinned against to varying degrees. To the ones for whom I wrote this book: You may have walked through times when someone has done despicable and unthinkable things to you. Trauma can result from a vast array of scenarios, and I want to be sensitive to you if you have been physically or mentally abused by another person. If you are currently in a situation that places you in harm's way, or you just came out of a situation like that, the authorities must be alerted. No one has the right to defile you, abuse you, or risk your life; no crime should ever be swept under the rug or hidden from the authorities. We have a justice system for a purpose, and none of us are above the law. The authorities must get involved so that justice according to the law can be established. Wanting to see justice served and enacted is not a bad thing. Our justice system is in place to protect our lives and our liberty, and if a law has been broken, we need to take action to begin the process toward justice.

That said, we are also to be freely forgiving people. We must hand them over to the law if they have committed a crime, but then we release them and lay our hurts, our cares, our worries, and our traumas at the feet of Jesus. We wash ourselves clean of any offense that has been birthed in us or allowed to take root in our hearts. Oh, believe me, this is as difficult for me to practice in real life as it is difficult for me to write about. The Lord has convicted me of this so often, as I described in a previous chapter. Even when I hear of harsh words spoken or written about me online, my first inclination is to fire back or defend myself. My heart loves justice, and I often desire to be vindicated somehow for all that has been done against me. But then conviction comes in, and I realize I am no better than anyone else from whom I seek recompense. I am a sinner, and I struggle each day. I am no better than the one who has sinned against me.

Our desire for justice should not cause us to wish harm on another person. This is what is difficult, because anger and the need for justice can bubble up out of us as an innate response. We want justice, and we want vindication. It is a part of our culture, and even deeper, it is part of our very nature, which can be seen throughout the Bible. The first instance of this is recorded in Genesis 4, in the story of Cain and Abel. They were brothers, but when Cain grew jealous of Abel and the favor that was upon him, Cain allowed anger to build up inside him, and he killed his brother, Abel. The Lord saw this, and He said to Cain, *"What have you done? The voice of your brother's blood is crying out to me from the ground"* (Gen. 4:10 nasb). The Lord cares for each and every one of His children, and He will demand recompense for sin in His own way.

Satan is the instigator of sin and division, and if we are not careful, he will use our bitterness and offenses toward other people against us. The Lord clearly says that we should love our enemies and bless those who curse us. How many of us have this mastered? None of us, right? There is a constant tug-of-war in our hearts on this issue, because our flesh wants to see justice served for the wrongs that have been done against us. But giving it to the Lord does not mean you are excusing their sin or brushing it under the rug; it is simply allowing the Lord to handle the situation.

I will say it again, however: If you have been physically harmed or a crime was committed, that must be handled by the authorities, and the justice system must get involved. Immediately begin to take all necessary steps, and be confident that the Lord is working for you through the systems that have been put in place for your safety. On the other hand, if you curse someone who curses you, you will not prosper. Jesus Himself tells us this in Matthew 6:14: *"For if you forgive others for their transgressions, your heavenly Father will also forgive you"* (nasb). When you pray, you will not gain any reward in that situation. If you pray for blessings to fall upon the one who hurt you, the result may mean a softer heart for them, their repentance, their turning themselves in and admitting their wrongs, or a deeper relationship with Jesus for that person. What might return to you? Those blessings will return with interest attached. What you freely give will be freely given to you.

Forgiveness is a weapon that completely confuses and obliterates the enemy. He does not expect us to bless those who intend harm to us, and he works hard to ensure that we retaliate. As retaliation is a part of our sin nature, resisting it requires a supernatural response from the Father. Satan even works in ways to heighten some situations and make things appear worse than they actually are. He works to distort our perceptions regarding the intentions of others, which creates a picture that might not be rooted in truth. We must be constantly renewing our minds to what is good and to what Jesus is doing, because we are in a constant battle—now more than ever.

I encourage you in this moment to write out any areas in which you have been harboring negative feelings, including those you have not forgiven, or where you may have any contempt for another person. Next to these names or areas of offense, write out a blessing for the person who hurt you; pray over that person and pray for freedom for yourself. Remember, no matter how badly someone has hurt you, they are also a child of God, and He loves them just as He loves you. Who better to intercede on their behalf than the person who has been wronged by them? Imagine the damage to hell that would create!

Forgiveness doesn't mean that we should not have clear boundaries or that we should become best friends with others who seek to harm us, but it does free us from partnering with the sin as well. Bless and release. It is time for many of us to be free once and for all, and sit at the table that the Lord has prepared for us.

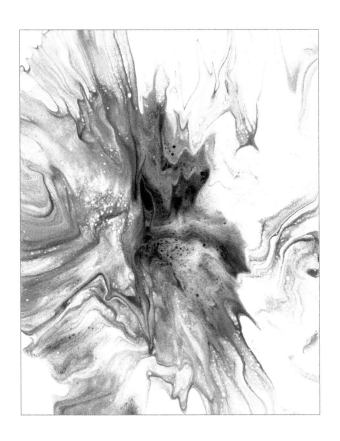

PRAISE IS A WEAPON

He Is Worthy to Be Praised

Shout for joy to the Lord, all the earth. Worship the Lord with gladness; come before him with joyful songs. Know that the Lord is God. It is he who made us, and we are his; we are his people, the sheep of his pasture. Enter his gates with thanksgiving and his courts with praise; give thanks to him and praise his name. For the Lord is good and his love endures forever; his faithfulness continues through all generations.

— PSALM 100:1–5 NIV

I have always been moved by music. My husband has learned that if I am in a bad mood, he can turn on nineties pop music, and it will immediately snap me out of my funk. I am laughing at that truth about me, because it is literally like a light switch for my mood. Music speaks to every cell in my body, and it gives me an instant recharge. Nineties music speaks to me because those are the songs of my childhood, and they bring back wonderful memories. I truly believe that God can use anything to speak to His children. Whether you have a musical talent or not, music is for everyone. I am a singer and a dancer who feels music in my soul.

I have always loved worshiping the Lord thorough song and movement, but it took on a new meaning and grew to deeper depths when God did something new in my life, when He healed me of trauma and all that went along with it. Now worshiping still means singing His praises, but it also means giving thanks, prayer, walking in the fruit of the Spirit, seeking to become more like Him, and inviting Him in all aspects of my life. It means coming into alignment with Him and living my life yielded to His ways.

Worshiping the Lord cannot be left for just a few songs on Sunday morning in a church service. Our everyday steps need to reflect our worship to the Lord. We may get knocked down again and again, but those who have eyes to see and ears to hear His voice, those who stay close to His heart through good times and bad, will continue to be lifted up and elevated by His Spirit. He will continue to walk with us and guide us through all things. Our relationship with Him begins with worship and praise for all He has done. He longs to be near us!

If you are walking through a battle, and then, in an instant, you are healed, rescued, and receive revelation of the Lord in a new way—worship is the first posture you should seek. In my life, it was a natural, innate response. I immediately knew what He had done for me, and I knew exactly to whom to give all glory and honor.

Here are some of my favorite worship verses. Try singing these to the Lord, or speak them aloud as you minister to Him. You can also search online or in your Bible to find other verses of praise and adoration to our good, good Father.

You, God, are my God, earnestly I seek you; I thirst for You, my whole being longs for You, in a dry and parched land where there is no water.

—PSALM 63:1 NIV

Praise be to the God and Father of our Lord Jesus Christ, the Father of compassion and the God of all comfort, who comforts us in all our troubles, so that we can comfort those in any trouble with the comfort we ourselves receive from God.

—2 CORINTHIANS 1:3–4 NIV

"How great you are, O Sovereign Lord! There is no one like you. We have never even heard of another God like you!"

—2 SAMUEL 7:22 NLT

Let everything that breathes sing praises to the Lord! Praise the Lord!

—PSALM 150:6 NLT

O Lord, You are my God; I will exalt You, I will give thanks to Your name; for You have worked wonders, plans formed long ago, with perfect faithfulness.

—ISAIAH 25:1 NASB

For from Him and through Him and to Him are all things. To Him be the glory forever. Amen.

—ROMANS 11:36 NASB

Why, my soul, are you downcast? Why so disturbed within me? Put your hope in God, for I will yet praise him, my Savior and my God.

—PSALM 42:11 NIV

Give praise to the Lord, proclaim his name; make known among the nations what he has done.

—PSALM 105:1 NIV

We Were Made to Worship

All the nations you have made will come and worship before you, Lord; they will bring glory to your name. For you are great and do marvelous deeds; you alone are God.

— PSALM 86:9–10 ESV

If you are new to living a life of worship toward God, I urge you to read the book of Psalms. The primary author of this book is King David. Even with his many failures, mistakes, and sins, God still called him "a man after My heart." David was a worshiper. He knew that he was nothing without the Lord, and God proved time and time again that He would show up and take action on David's behalf. The life of David is one we can likely relate to. He was not shy about the turmoil he faced and crying out to God "*where are you?*" when it seemed that God was not near. The aspect of David that I appreciate is that through his honesty of what He was facing in life, by the end of the Psalm, He was praising the Lord for who He was and who He is and what promises were yet to come. Worshipping the Father changes the way we see a situation and it shows us the heart of God and breaks any stronghold preventing us from hearing the Lord.

You, too, were made to worship the Lord. The gifts He has given you to carry are launching moments for how He wants to partner with you. No one else has your special gifts. You are uniquely created and loved by the Almighty God. Competing with other people or feeling like you have missed your chance or that you have messed up too greatly will not take away your kingdom assignment. You were made to come into divine alignment with heaven and the blood of Jesus, and then step into the areas into which God is calling you—but *you* have to step into it. It will not just come to you. As you step out in faith, you will see that specific aspects of your assignment will become straightforward, resources will become available, elements that must be left behind will be unveiled, and knowledge and wisdom regarding your path will start to become comprehensible. Be confident that the Lord is moving on your behalf and as you continue to move forward, He will meet you and exceed your greatest dreams.

It all starts with reverence for God. In the Lord's Prayer, Jesus instructed us to begin with the phrase, "Our Father, who is in heaven, hallowed be Your name." The meaning of *hallowed* in Hebrew is "to be set apart or greatly revered and honored" (*Oxford Dictionary*, 2020). One synonym for *hallowed* is "to be worshiped" (*Meriam-Webster Thesaurus*, 2020). We are not on the same level as God, and when we see ourselves in His presence, it is glaringly obvious that there is a vast divide in our worthiness to even be near Him. What is so beautiful; however, is that despite our failures, shortcomings, and character flaws, He wants us to know Him, to come to His table and be in fellowship with Him. We do this with humble praise, knowing that we could never pay for ourselves what Jesus paid for.

The Godhead—comprised of the Father, the Son, Jesus, and the Holy Spirit—are worthy to be praised, and it is our honor to do so when we remember where we came from, what we were delivered from, who paid the price for our salvation, and that this free gift can never be repaid. Understanding grace only comes into full perspective when we feel the depths of it and know that we are completely unmerited for receiving such a wonderful gift. We have favor in the eyes of the Lord despite our wicked ways, our sinful desires, and hateful hearts. He gave this freely and He died to save all, even having full knowledge that many would not freely choose Him.

We know the Lord by the many names that He calls Himself throughout the Bible. The one that I keep hearing in my spirit over and over again is Elohim. *Elohim* means "God of might; mighty Creator; Almighty God" (*NAS Exhaustive Concordance of the Bible with Hebrew-Aramaic and Greek Dictionaries*, 1998). It is the first name of God that is used in the Bible when He is described as the Creator of all things. Genesis 1:1 states: "*In the beginning God created the heavens and the earth*" (niv). When the Bible was translated into English, all the many names of God were simply translated to "God," but the translation from the Hebrew for the Genesis 1:1 is *Elohim*. Elohim is also the most frequently used name for God used in the Bible. He is almighty, powerful, and majestic. He is the supreme deity and the Creator of all things, the mighty innovator and genius in all things. As it says in

Isaiah 40:28: *"Have you never heard? Have you never understood? The Lord is the everlasting God, the Creator of all the earth"* (nlt).

We are miracles created by a miracle-working Father. He is still on the move, working on our behalf, and He is looking for the ones who want to co-create with Him. It does not matter what background you came from, the family you were born into, the circumstances and hardships you have faced, or the sins you have committed. He has provided everything you need out of absolute love for you. He deserves all our honor and praise because it is a miracle that we even make it through most days. The air we breathe is a miracle, and the fact that our body functions the way that it does is a miracle. Every life created in the womb is a miracle, and *you* are a miracle. What He wants to do through you in signs, wonders, and miracles is not difficult for Him because He is the Creator of all things.

The Lord Is with You, Mighty Warrior

As they began to sing and praise, the Lord set ambushes against the men of Ammon and Moab and Mount Seir who were invading Judah, and they were defeated.

— 2 CHRONICLES 20:22 NIV

Fear is in overabundance where trauma lives, and it tends to be the driving force for the enemy to play games against our minds, and at times, in how we react to situations. Sometimes it might feel like the enemy is closing in, pushing you into a corner, which forces a response. For me, when I felt pushed into a corner or that something was closing in on me, I would respond with yelling and outbursts of anger to get it to stop. It was sort of like sounding an alarm, and the sound of my voice was the blast. I am not proud of using this defense mechanism, especially when it was directed toward the wrong target, but I no longer feel shame about that. My reactions were grounded in pain and fear, and came from unclean places, but the principle and the potential of goodness was a seed that was always in me. Being pressed on all sides like that has a way of revealing aspects about our character that are not godly, but we know that God always uses what was meant for bad, for good. So, what if those character "flaws" are just misdirected gifts?

I am going to shift here in order to round out my thought process. Let me tell you a story from the Bible, one of my absolute favorites and one that I relate to on deep levels. It is the story of a man who was defeated, who was alone, and who felt unworthy. Israel had sinned greatly against God after He rescued them from Egypt. They had disobeyed God's law by worshiping the gods of the land they now inhabited. As a result, God allowed them to be severely oppressed. All of the crops they would grow were overtaken, and they were relentlessly mistreated, finding themselves once again enslaved. They would hide in caves for safety and shelter.

This is the story of Gideon in the book of Judges 6–7. Gideon was visited by an angel of the Lord who spoke to Gideon's identity and destiny—due to how God saw him, not how he saw himself. This is so profound, because God will always speak to you according to your identity and who He created you to be. He does this to show you that you are not where you are supposed to be, to invite you deeper into a relationship, and to elevate you into the place of authority for which you were created as a co-heir of Christ.

The angel greeted Gideon by saying, *"The Lord is with you, mighty warrior"* (Judg. 6:12 nasb). Gideon's response is one we all have had from time to time: *"Pardon me, my lord,"* Gideon replied, *"but if the Lord is with us, why has all this happened to us?"* (verse 13 nasb). Isn't this a question that many of us find ourselves asking? "Why do You allow bad things to happen, Lord?" Have you found yourself hindering all forward progression as you seek the answer to that question? The Lord freely responds to us and our questions, but in my experience, He does not typically answer this particular question. I believe that God does not want us to focus on the question of why, but instead He wants us to partner with Him in a situation. Instead of asking why He would allow something to happen, what if we responded with, "What are You saying in this moment, Lord, and what can I do?"

Gideon's story continues with the Lord's response in verse 14: *"Go in the strength you have and save Israel out of Midian's hand. Am I not sending you?"* (nasb). We might not be the strongest person physically, and we may be broken emotionally, but the Lord loves to use people who are in situations just like this to prove that it could only be the work of the Lord. He told Gideon to go as he was and with what he had—which was very little. But the Lord's promise to Gideon was that He would save Israel, and that He was going to equip Gideon with what he needed to get the job done.

Have you ever tried to talk God out of something? I began this book by telling you that the Lord had told me He was going to anoint me to write books. My initial response was, "You must have the wrong person." That was exactly Gideon's response, too. The Lord reassures us that He will be with us always, and that was His direct promise to Gideon. All of God's promises are *"yes and amen"* (2 Cor. 2:20 niv). We can hold on to these promises with absolute victory because God does not fail. This does not mean that there will not be adversaries who will try to steal that promise. In fact, I would propose that if you have an assurance from the Lord, you can expect spiritual attacks to ramp up exponentially for a few different reasons. I believe they are to derail you from fulfilling God's mandate on your life, to which many of us have been subjected. We have been delayed because we have allowed the enemy to lie to us for so long that we have believed it as a fact. Everything that we have grown up believing should be addressed with Christ and filtered through the cross. Ask the Lord if what was said is true, or if it is the Truth. There is a difference. The world can come up with circumstantial evidence and present "facts" that all line up to be "true." Many people will cling onto their own "truth," based on their thoughts, emotions, and beliefs. But we know that our thoughts, emotions, and wills are not always reliable. There is only one absolute Truth, and that is Jesus. Even if aspects of the Bible make us uncomfortable and confront certain beliefs on to which we have held, our emotional wrestling with the Word of God versus what we have held on to as belief will always be severed by the Truth of the Lord. We must remain open and willing to learn more of what God is saying through His Word.

An interesting aspect about Gideon was that he wanted to know that what he was doing was God's will and not from the enemy that was at work in the land, something he had imagined, or something that came from his own desires. His people had turned away from God and were participating in the sinful ways of this world and had a mixed culture of the ways of God and the ways of the flesh. Perhaps Gideon had allowed skepticism to arise in his heart when the Lord came upon him while familiar spirit of enslavement rose up in him. Battling two worlds causes confusion when attempting to decipher truth. If he were wrong with hearing from God, it would put his family, his entire community, and his nation at risk of annihilation, so you can imagine the weight of what was being asked of him. So, the Lord allowed Gideon to test Him, asking for confirming signs that it was without a doubt the Lord who was asking him to go on this mission. The Lord was patient and merciful with Gideon because the Lord knew the warrior that Gideon was going to be and He needed someone, despite where they were on their walk with the Lord, to rise up, If the Lord is not upon us and within us, then we will inevitably fall. It is a dangerous road to "test" the Lord, however. There are many verses in the Bible that confirm that. Jesus said to His disciples, *"It is said, 'You shall not put the LORD your God to the test'"* (Lk 4:12 niv).

Just as Moses led the Israelites out of Egypt in Exodus 12 and 13, they immediately went into the "wilderness" season. They needed to rid themselves of the culture from which they came. Gideon was experiencing the same thing. He was intertwined into a culture that was sacrificing to false gods, but the Lord had an acceleration on Gideon. There was an urgency and the Lord showed mercy and kindness to Gideon, much like how He has done for me.

When we have lived our entire lives believing and experiencing one way, and suddenly that all comes crashing down, we are going to need a grace period. Naturally we might be hesitant to just believe everything we see or hear. The Lord tells us to *"test everything; hold fast what is good"* (1 Thess. 5:21 esv). Gideon was not demanding God in a way to have authority over him; he was earnestly wanting to encounter the one true Lord and his faith was not strong. The requests being made needed to be tested so that it would build his faith, so he could hold on to what was true and good, as it would give him strength to complete the task. I believe that when things on our journey get hard, when adversaries show up, or when someone tells you that you cannot do something that you have tested and proven to be good and true, you can hold tightly to those promises and declare them over your situation to defeat the enemy trying to hold you back. Faith is a shield and weapon of warfare against attacks from the enemy.

We later learn in Judges 7 that Gideon rounded up his army. He knew that he was going to be heading into a battle, and he needed manpower. The Lord spoke to Gideon in verse 2 and 3, saying, *"You have too many men. I cannot deliver Midian into their hands, or Israel would boast against Me, 'My own strength has saved me.' Now announce to the army, 'Anyone who trembles with fear may turn back and leave Mount Gilead.'" So twenty-two thousand men left, while ten thousand remained"* (nasb).

If Gideon had gone into the enemy camp with 32,000 men, he surely would have had the manpower to defeat them by their own will and power. But that is not what God wanted to do. God is the God of signs and wonders, and He wanted to make it absolutely clear that He is the one true God. So, Gideon's army was decreased by over half. The Lord interjected again, saying, "Hey, Gideon, this still is not going to work for Me. Your army is still too big." So, the army was whittled down to merely three hundred men.

Finally, orders came to Gideon from the Lord that now was the time, but He was so incredibly kind and merciful to Gideon. He knew that Gideon was afraid, but God needed Gideon to have incredibly bold faith to complete the task, so He told Gideon to go down to the enemy's camp. When Gideon did so, he was able to listen to the enemy troops reveal the wild dreams they were having of a giant loaf of bread coming down the hill and annihilating their camp. The Lord allowed them to interpret the dream—and the only answer that was given was that the sword of Gideon was going to overtake them. When Gideon heard this interpretation of their dream, he immediately fell down in worship to the Lord.

Have you ever been given a confirmation from the Lord about something, especially something that seemed so far-fetched that you tried to dismiss it as a mistake or a figment of your imagination? These moments when God confirms something He said fill us with faith, power, might, belief, and great strength. This is the Lord's way of showing us He is for us and that He is with us. This moment gave Gideon the greatest momentum of His journey because He had tested God before, and he had become well acquainted with the presence of God and His mighty works. As we become aware of the voice of God in our own lives, we become more aware of when He speaks. It grows overtime as any relationship does and we can all get to a place that when the Lord speaks, we immediately acknowledge it.

This was the only validation and vindication Gideon needed. He rose up with strength and declared to his men that it was time for them to rise up. Uncommon war weapons are our praise and a shout. Many times throughout the Bible, the Lord has used sound, shouts, songs of praise, and instruments as war weapons. He gave Gideon and his army trumpets, which carried the sound of heaven, and jars. Gideon divided up the three hundred men into three companies, and they surrounded the enemies camp. At Gideon's order, they broke the jars, which was a prophetic act that signifies we as believers being broken before the Lord. He is the potter and we are the clay (Isa. 64:8), and the significance of breaking the jars is our willingness to be broken for Him. He wants to dismantle everything we have built above Him, to break any covenant we have had with false gods and idols. We must allow Him into those broken spaces to fill and to mend.

Gideon's army then sounded their trumpets and shouted, "*A sword for the Lord and for Gideon!*" (Judg. 7:20 nasb). When three hundred trumpets sounded all at once, can you comprehend the sound? Imagine if they carried a supernatural sound, a war cry and decree from heaven. What followed was the fulfillment of the prophetic dream that Gideon heard. The enemy camp was filled with fear and terror, and they turned on each other and began killing one another.

I told you that story to say this: The Lord told me that He is raising up modern-day Gideons who will carry a sound from heaven. I believe that these people—maybe you who are reading this—will be renewed in their identity to Christ, despite being told that their character flaws could never be useful for kingdom purposes. I believe my outbursts of yelling were a misdirected gift from heaven that was not being used for its intended purpose. I was using my gift to shout in the wrong direction, due to lies and deceit from the enemy. Once I got back into alignment with the Lord and turned the opposite way, the Lord gave me a shout, a war cry that would make hell quake. It is not by my will, not by my might, but by the Lord.

I have confidence that the Lord wants to use you in the same way in this time right now. Once you find that area that Satan has been highlighting and using to bring you shame, and you give it to God, He will use it as a weapon to destroy Satan and his entire army. The sound that will come from the modern-day Gideons will cause the army of the enemy to turn on itself and fall to their demise. Remember, we are not talking about people, or flesh and blood. We fight and war in the spirit against principalities, evil spirits, and hell itself.

Arise, you mighty warriors, the Lord is with you! It is time to release the sound of heaven!

Prayer

Father,

Thank You, Elohim, for creating us and for Your desire to intimately know us. We realize that we are not worthy of Your affections or salvation. We humbly enter into Your presence with the fear of You, Lord, the fear of Your absence. Thank You for Jesus, for sending Your Son to bear our sin and shame and for washing us clean with the blood of the Lamb. Father, I ask that the person who is reading this right now would be washed afresh this day. I pray that repentance of old sins would occur, and that she would turn from her old ways and seek Your face. I pray that from the top of her head to the bottom of her feet, she would feel Your love and Your fresh anointing dripping off of her now, in the name of Jesus. You are worthy of all our praise, and we lift You up, King of kings and Lord of lords, our Savior, our Creator, our Healer, and our Deliverer. Nothing is impossible for You, Lord. I break off every chain that is holding this dear reader down. Throw open the prison gates and bring healing to the hearts, minds, and spirits of Your daughter right now in the name of Jesus. I pray that this warrior would arise with a sound from heaven that will scramble and confuse the plans of hell, and that all attacks against her would be sent back to where they came from. We bring our thanksgiving to You. We sing Your praises, and for all that was and is to come, we thank You, Jesus. Amen and amen.

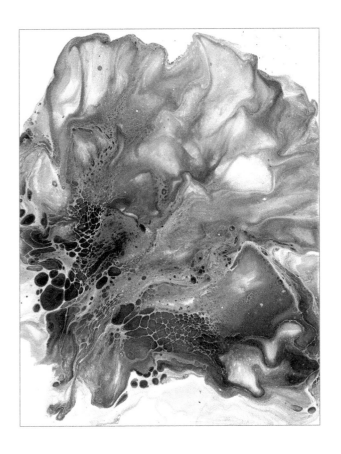

TESTIMONIES HEAL

Testimonies Build Faith

At this I fell at his feet to worship him. But he said to me, "Don't do that! I am a fellow servant with you and with your brothers and sisters who hold to the testimony of Jesus. Worship God! For it is the Spirit of prophecy who bears testimony to Jesus."

— REVELATION 19:10 NIV

I recently went to a church conference where a massive number of people were receiving physical healing just through other people's testimonies. One lady had suffered with back issues for many decades, which impeded her quality of life. She told the story that through prayer and the laying on of hands, she had made a miraculous full recovery. As she was telling her story, someone in the audience who apparently had been dealing with the same or a similar condition for most of her life, had a miraculous healing right there on the spot!

Our testimonies have the ability to create miracles for other people. They have the ability to build up someone else's faith. If the Lord healed you of your ailment, and it was the same ailment I suffered with, I would be very interested in your story, and hope, faith, and belief would arise in me as I began to believe that might happen for me as well. Stepping out in faith and having belief as small as a mustard seed is referenced many times in the Bible.

One of my favorite stories is the woman with the issue with bleeding, found in Mark 5. It was unlawful for this woman to be out in the community around other people. If she encountered someone by accident, she was supposed to announce that she was unclean so that they could avoid her. My heart hurts for this woman, who was extremely isolated and constantly humiliated. It's unlikely that she was able to do much or make any wages, so she likely lived a very impoverished life as well.

She had heard testimonies about Jesus and the many miracles that were happening to everyone He touched, including people who were considered unclean, as she was. She was in a desperate place, and maybe she thought she had nothing to lose. If she could just touch the hem of Jesus' garment, maybe it would be enough, and no one would see her breaking the law. She defied the written law and left her home, stepping out in faith to touch the hem of His garment. As she did, Jesus felt power leave His body.

That is what happens when we step out in faith. It activates the power of Jesus within us for miracles to happen. Mark 5:34 tells us: *"He said to her, 'Daughter, your faith has healed you. Go in peace and be freed from your suffering'"* (nasb).

You do not owe anything for your divine healing. Jesus paid the full price for any and all diseases at the cross, including the effects of trauma. When the Lord told me to write "our story" (not "my story," because without Him, there is no power; saying "our" refers to the Lord and myself), He said telling the story would break chains and bring divine healing to those who have suffered trauma. I believe that, and I have a lot of faith in that for a few different reasons. I myself received supernatural, miraculous healing in this area in my life.

My depression, shame, doubt, anger, sorrow, anxiety, panic, and physical ailments were miraculously healed. In two months following my healing, I lost over thirty pounds. The Lord told me the weight I lost was the weight of the trauma I was carrying. Once the trauma was broken, so was the stronghold the weight had on me. All the pain from the physical ailments I was experiencing were miraculously gone at that moment as well. I have heard of other people who have been healed of similar traumas who also experienced supernatural weight loss. Sometimes the extra weight we carry is emotional or spiritual.

Another reason I have such belief and faith in sharing testimonies is because I have seen with my own eyes another person receive healing just from someone testifying to what the Lord has done. Our testimony is the Spirit of prophecy and declaring what the Lord has done is prophesying that it can happen for someone else (Rev. 19:10).

Lastly, another reason I have faith in the testimony is because I believe the written Word of God in its entirety, even if I do not understand some verses or I am tested in some way. Jesus' entire ministry was grounded on healing the sick and casting out devils, to allow people to feel the love and the power of the living God. There is nothing like being touched by the Father and receiving healing in something you have battled against that had caused pain, discomfort, and trials of all kinds. One moment with God will flip your life upside down in the best possible way. He desires to heal you and set you free!

Testimonies Bring Comfort

Wherefore comfort yourselves together, and edify one another, even as also ye do.

— *1 Thessalonians 5:11 kjv*

Knowing we are not alone in our journey with God brings hope and comfort. We were made to be in fellowship and community so that we could elevate, edify, and sharpen one another. Proverbs 27:17 states, *"As iron sharpens iron, so a friend sharpens a friend"* (nlt). As we learn through our own personal journey, we can help others and receive from God as they grow. God loves families and relationships, and He wants to restore the areas in our lives in which these aspects are broken. He does this by bringing comfort. I realize that not all family relationships are comforting, edifying, or even safe. Our society is plagued with abuse within the family, brokenness in marriages, and trauma caused by those to whom we are the closest in this life. This is yet another tactic of the enemy to steal and destroy God's divine plan for us. We might not get all the answers on this side of life as to why certain things happened to us or to those whom we love, but when we love God and seek Him, we encounter Him, and that is where peace and comfort are found.

We will become paralyzed if we focus on dissecting the reason a situation or circumstance occurred. This does not build faith—it only increases doubt. I am a thinker, and so I am always trying to analyze scenarios, but each time I turn my attention toward the problem, I get derailed in my emotions. That will eventually separate my attention from Jesus, and when I let go of His hand, most of the time I do not even realize what has happened. I am completely turned the other way until I am again in a troubling matter and need rescue.

Thankfully, we not only have the ultimate comforter in the Holy Spirit, but He gave us each other. I do not have a huge circle of people, but the ones whom the Lord has sent me have been wonderful sharpening tools for me. They help to keep me straight on my path on my personal walk with Jesus.

Testimonies Break Chains

They triumphed over him by the blood of the Lamb and by the word of their testimony; they did not love their lives so much as to shrink from death.

— REVELATION 12:11 NIV

Nothing can withstand the power of the blood. No evil thing—no stronghold, no weapon formed against you, no abuse, no sexual sin done to you, no power of hell—can resist the power of the blood of Jesus. Everything that you have been through in your life is repairable. Every sin you have committed is forgivable. Jesus loves you so much that He died for you. He gave you all of His power and authority to trample on anything that would come to devour you. He wants your shackles to wither like dust before your very eyes. He wants to remove the burden of what you are carrying and instead place a crown upon your head and a mantle over your shoulders. I can just imagine Him saying, *"We have so much work to do. Are you ready? It is going to be so much fun!"*

I write these words to encourage you and give you hope to see what is possible in partnering with Almighty God. You may have been contending for healing for a long time. Maybe you tried everything and have thought, "Maybe God does not want to set me free." I get it. I was there myself for a long time. I asked many people to pray over me, I completed all the Bible studies, and I read book after book, trying to find the "secret sauce" to healing, freedom, and deliverance. There had to be more to this life than suffering, right?

We were not promised an easy life, but we were promised peace despite calamity around us for those living for the Lord. Living in the aftermath of trauma is usually the opposite of peace, and I know for a fact that is not the journey God intended for anyone. If you have gotten this far in this book, I hope that you now see that your healing journey, your broken chains, and your strongholds hinge on your identity in Christ Jesus. Who do you think you are, and to whom do you belong? You were made for a purpose, and every pain you have suffered was not the will or plan of God. Still, He will use them as a counter weapon to defeat hell on your behalf.

Our outlook on our present trouble changes significantly when we get into divine alignment with Elohim. God is raising up His army, and He needs His daughters to stand in their authority. He loves each of us more than we will ever know, and even if we walk in great intimacy with Him, He loves to surprise us with new ways to tell us how much He adores us and exactly what we mean to Him. Sometimes our faith and stepping out will break the chains. Other times He might send someone to us with a word of knowledge about our situation that they would not otherwise know, to let us know exactly who we are and how beloved we are to our Creator.

It astounds me that despite how tiny I am in the grand scheme of this universe, God still desires my heart. Out of all the people in this world, He has a plan to use me for His kingdom. He wants to use me to help bring healing to others who have gone through similar trials. Freedom is freely available, and there are others just like you and me who are the remnants of Christ. They have gone through catastrophe and are willing to arise and use their testimony to bring other people to freedom as well.

Imagine the army of healed and equipped daughters whom God wants to use for the kingdom of God. Imagine all of these warriors rising up from the ashes, dusting themselves off, and remembering that once again, or perhaps for the very first time, who they truly are. Sometimes we know who we are, but life events happen and we stop fighting, losing track of who we really are.

Maybe attacks came your way in an effort to silence what God had planned for you. Suddenly, the Lord will come upon you, and in an instant you will recognize the sound, you will recognize the face, the smell, and the feeling of His presence upon you. So, rise up, and the chains and strongholds will wither up and blow away in the wind. Draw your sword and speak the Word of the Lord.

Imagine if all the Father's daughters in this land did this very thing? Imagine the damage we could do to the kingdom of darkness, just by stepping into our identity and aligning ourselves with what heaven wants to do on the earth right now!

ACTIVATED

I have provided some easy, practical activation exercises throughout this book. I would encourage you to go back and rehearse the decrees, reflect on the devotions, and practice the five-by-three devotionals that I mentioned in chapter 12 (where you pray for five minutes, write for five minutes, and read the Bible for five minutes). These are not a definitive or absolute approach to hearing the voice of God for yourself, but they worked for me, and I encourage you to give them a try. There are so many great activation exercises available online for free, if you do a simple internet search; that will also help you grow in this area. (What I mean by "activation" is simply practicing the use of all your senses to encounter the Lord.)

Just like any skill that we learn—such as learning a new subject or concept in school; on-the-job training; practicing singing, dancing, or playing a musical instrument; or anything else you are attempting to grow more proficient in—honing the gifts and skills God has given to us must be practiced in the same way.

I do not want you to worry about missing it, messing up, or failing. That is just part of the process. When you seek the face of God and step out in faith, sometimes you will miss it. Listen for any corrections or guidance that the Lord is speaking to you through journaling and through fellowship with other believers as you help to sharpen each other. When you learn what is coming from your flesh versus the Father's will, eventually you will grow accustomed to knowing when the Lord speaks and you can partner with that. It takes time, and maybe you are just coming out of a difficult situation or you are still contending for your healing. Use these activations to minister to the Lord. Read aloud to Him the scriptures and decrees. Sing the scriptures to Him in adoration. Ask Him questions for revelation and ask Him to show you what He is saying about a situation. Ask Him what He wants to do and how you can walk with Him on your journey. Tell Him what you are struggling with and ask for the spirit of knowledge and wisdom. The more you seek the Father's heart, the more you will encounter Him. Just as in any relationship, it takes work. You still go on dates with your spouse or make time for one another, and it is the same, if not more important, regarding your relationship with the Lord. We are His bride, and He wants interaction, oneness, and intimacy with us.

Get into the Word

I have never been successful at doing the Bible-in-a-year study plans or reading the Bible through in chronological order. I find that if I put strict parameters on my time with the Lord, it becomes too legalistic, or I practice it out of regiment instead of connection. Then I tend to get down on myself if I miss a day, and I attempt to make it up at a later time. This does not adequately allow me to meditate on a smaller chunk at a time—and I miss things that way. Sometimes God just gives me one verse and has me read it over and over again, emphasizing a different word each time I read it. Then I write it down, memorize it, make it into a decree, and chew and digest it as He reveals His heart to me.

I like to use my time with the Lord as a way to learn how to communicate with Him and allow Him to communicate back to me, so I typically ask Him to give me a Scripture reference of where He wants me to start, or sometimes I just open to a random page and pray for the Holy Spirit to speak to me through the Word at that time—to help me understand what He is saying, how the Word is relevant to me and my life situations, and what He wants me to do with this word from Him. Does He want me to use a passage to pray and intercede on the behalf of someone else? Does He want to circumcise my heart and fill me with His bread for sustenance? Does He want to challenge a false belief that I have partnered with and reveal to me His ultimate Truth? I welcome it all, and I am open and willing to let Him take the lead.

If it is more beneficial for you to do a study or use a regimented plan, then please do so. However you feel comfortable and however God loves to speak to you individually is very important. My methods described throughout this book are solely based on my experiences and encounters with the Lord. I know that it might be easier for you if I just told you exactly how growing in the Lord is done, and then you can get to work doing that for yourself, but God made us each unique, with different skill sets and strengths. He wants to highlight to you your own personal, unique ways of learning, seeing, and hearing—and that is likely very different from mine.

There is nothing wrong if you approach things differently or if the Lord wants to speak to you in visions or dreams or through other people. The way you encounter the Lord today might look differently next year to you, too, so it is vital that you stay committed to seeking His face and not growing offended at the way He chooses to move or communicate with you. My intention is for you to learn that who you are in relationship to God matters and to provide you with sample tools on how to proceed from there. Take them at face value or use them as a launching pad to grow with Jesus on your own terms.

Step Out in Faith and Forgive

I know forgiveness is hard, especially when someone has done something terribly wrong to you or someone you love. But friend, forgiveness is a weapon that the Lord can use in the war room and move mightily on your behalf. Justice is His and His alone. If you do not forgive, then you cannot be forgiven. I know this could be hard to hear, and if I had read these words a few years ago, I would have challenged them or maybe felt a little upset. We tend to want to see justice served, but our fight is not with other people. We must remember that there is a real enemy that works through people in various ways. We fight against those principalities and pray for freedom for the ones who are used as instruments of destruction in Jesus' name.

I am greatly moved by justice being served to the enemy. I am a warrior, but while watching the enemy tuck his tail and run is glorious, it is ultimately not my battle. It is the Lord's. It has already been finished, it has already been written, and justice is and will eventually be served. When we are seated in heavenly places and can see our situations from a kingdom perspective, we can easily forgive because we see the big gap between us and God and we realize that we ourselves have been freely forgiven of many sins.

When we look away from the act of what someone has done and instead look at their broken soul, we can then forgive and even intercede for them, praying that they also will radically encounter the Lord. I am not saying this is easy or that I always get this right. But we can always try again and repent of our partnership with the situation—not that we are at fault in the relationship breach, but if we are refusing to forgive, we are partnering with the sin.

Also, we do not brush anything under the rug—remember that. We take it to the throne room and state our case. If it is a situation in which a crime has been committed and the authorities need to get involved, then we must take action and pray for God to bring swift justice in the natural. This is a way that we can partner with God. We don't let things slide, but we do not use the justice of God simply because we do not agree with an individual, the way they are living, or the choices they make for themselves or their families. We do not wish ill to be done to anyone, and we do not curse anyone. There is mighty power in the tongue; it can be used for God's purposes or Satan's agenda, so we must always be vigilant as to which narrative we are declaring. Allow the justice system to work as it should, then wash the burden off of you by the cleansing blood of Jesus.

We can do all of this by prayers of repentance and thanksgiving, and by placing the burden at the feet of Jesus. There is no law against walking in the fruit of the Spirit. No one can falsely accuse you, no one can rightly jail you, and no one can harm you if you are walking in the fruit of the Spirit. This is the obvious evidence that God resides in you and is working through you.

Final Notes

Sister, I pray that the Lord has touched your heart as you read this book, and I pray that it challenged you to see things from a different perspective and open your heart for healing. Now more than ever, we need one another as sisters in Christ to lift one another up and sharpen each other with absolute Truth from the Word of God. As I mentioned earlier, these are my interpretations and what I have felt to write during my personal moments with the Father. I urge you to test my words and seek the Lord for yourself. Practice the activations, look up the Bible references, meditate on them, and allow the Father to encounter you in a new way—or maybe for the first time ever.

If you get knocked down, I urge you to stand up again—and keep on standing up as many times as it takes. Allow perseverance to be instilled in you so that you will grow in maturity and knowledge. Keep walking in His ways, even if you fail over and over again. He will meet you where you are, and He will bless you on your journey to seek repentance and His ways. His mercy and goodness are so good, and I pray that you feel His presence and His hope even in the midst of trials of all kinds. I release peace to enter your spirit as you learn your identity as a child of God. I pray that you feel the peace that makes no sense in light of all that you face.

As I was seeking the Lord while writing the conclusion of this book, He told me to finish it with a love letter to you, His dear daughter. The love for you that He allowed me to feel had me on my face in worship, because He is so merciful! This kind of love is not an earthly love that I can adequately describe. I have been wrecked by how beautiful you are to Him.

In the Spirit, so vast across this world, I saw crowds of the Father's beautiful daughters grouped together. They filled the cities, the regions, the states, and the nations. Then God zoomed me out, and I saw them covering the entire earth in every nation raising their swords high above their heads. He loves all of His daughters as a group, but also so uniquely and individually. He is with you mighty warriors.

Here is a love letter from your Father God, what I heard Him speaking to the collective body of daughters in this time. I pray it blesses you as it blessed me.

My darling daughters,

You are precious in My eyes, says the Lord your God. Nothing can separate My love from you. I cannot wait for what we are about to do together. I always knew this day would come. I am delighted in you—I always have been. No one can steal what I have given to you. While Satan may have taken something from you that you thought you had lost forever, he will give you back all that he has stolen. I am going to make him pay it back and then some. Do not look at what is going on in the world around you; look farther out on the horizon, because the chaos around you is not from Me. Keep looking at the horizon, because what is coming is so good it is going to seem unbelievable. It will require you to focus on it out in the distance, to stand strong and steadfast, and to believe for it to come to pass. It is for you and for all of My children who keep standing on My promises.

Just like Gideon, you will be renewed in strength, and this will allow you to defeat what has come against you once and for all—because of your steadfast and unshakable faith and your partnership with Me, your ultimate Provider. Nothing is too big for Me. I love to show off for My children, and I will move mightily on your behalf. Keep pressing in and ask for more—more of the ability to hear and see Me, more healing, more of My presence, and more miracles. Keep knocking, keep seeking, and keep asking! What you may see as a delay in response is not a delay to Me. All of my promises are yes and amen!

Keep pressing in, for that is where you will find Me. I love you, darling daughters. You are so precious in My sight. Arise, dear ones. Now is the time for freedom, the time for you to take your seat in heavenly places.

Thank you, dear friend, for sticking with me through to the end of this book. I thank Almighty God for His wisdom in this project. All glory goes to Him! I leave you with this:

"Arise [from spiritual depression to a new life], shine [be radiant with the glory and brilliance of the Lord]; for your light has come, and the glory and brilliance of the Lord has risen upon you. For in fact, darkness will cover the earth and deep darkness will cover the peoples; but the Lord will rise upon you [Jerusalem] and His glory and brilliance will be seen on you. Nations will come to your light, and kings to the brightness of your rising."

—Isaiah 60:1–3 AMP

References

"Complacency." *Thesaurus by Merriam-Webster, 2020.* https://www.merriam-webster.com/thesaurus/complacency (3 January, 2020).

Easton, Matthew George. *Easton's Bible Dictionary.* New York: T. Nelson and Sons, 1894.

Orr, James, ed. *International Standard Bible Encyclopedia.* Grand Rapids, MI: Wm. B. Eerdmans Publishing Co., 1939.

Stevenson, Angus. *Oxford Dictionary of English (3rd ed.).* Oxford University Press, 2015.

Strong, James. *Strong's Expanded Exhaustive Concordance of the Bible.* Nashville: Thomas Nelson, 2009.

Thomas, Robert L., and W. Don Wilkins. *"New American Standard Exhaustive Concordance of the Bible: Hebrew-Aramaic and Greek Dictionaries."* Amazon Foundation Publications, 1998.

About the Author

Melissa Sanders has been a registered nurse since 2011, spending her career as an operating room nurse. Melissa loves researching the ways the body works to heal itself, and she educates people on natural modalities to help assist the body in doing that. She holds a bachelor's degree in kinesiology and has spent over a decade as a group fitness instructor. Her desire to write came from an encounter with the Lord, and she felt the prompting to share her story.

CPSIA information can be obtained
at www.ICGtesting.com
Printed in the USA
LVHW050909161220
674218LV00006B/120

9 781647 734862